Gender and Agency

for Maisie

Gender and Agency

Reconfiguring the Subject in Feminist and Social Theory

Lois McNay

Polity Press

First published in 2000 by Polity Press in association with Blackwell Publishers Ltd.

Editorial office:
Polity Press
65 Bridge Street
Cambridge CB2 1UR, UK

Marketing and production:
Blackwell Publishers Ltd
108 Cowley Road
Oxford OX4 1JF, UK

Published in the USA by
Blackwell Publishers Inc.
Commerce Place
350 Main Street
Malden, MA 02148, USA

A catalogue record for this book is available from the British Library.

Library of Congress Cataloging-in-Publication Data

McNay, Lois.
    Gender and agency : reconfiguring the subject in feminist and social theory /
Lois McNay.
        p.   cm.
    Includes bibliographical references and index.
    ISBN 0–7456–1348–9 (hc. : acid-free paper) — ISBN 0–7456–1349–7
(pbk. : acid-free paper)
    1. Feminist theory.   2. Sex role.   3. Gender identity.   4. Man-woman
relationships.   I. Title.

HQ1190.M393   2000
305.3—dc21   99–056202

Typeset in 11 on 13 pt Berling
by Graphicraft Limited, Hong Kong
Printed in Great Britain by MPG Books Ltd, Bodmin, Cornwall

This book is printed on acid-free paper.

CONTENTS

Acknowledgements

I would like to thank the following for their comments on parts of the manuscript at various stages in its drafting: Gráinne de Búrca, Michael Freeden, Bridget Fowler, Desmond King, Morny Joy, Nicola Lacey, John Thompson and Robert Young. I have benefited enormously from the support and friendship of Gráinne de Búrca. Kinch Hoekstra's patient discussion with me of various issues and his perceptive reading of sections of the manuscript were extremely helpful in clarifying my thoughts. Above all, I would like to thank Henrietta Moore, whose comments and insights were invaluable to the completion of this book.

I am indebted to the British Academy and Somerville College, Oxford, for their support in the form of research leave.

Parts of chapter 2 originally appeared in a revised form as 'Gender, Habitus and the Field: Pierre Bourdieu and the Limits of Reflexivity', *Theory, Culture and Society*, 16 (1): 95–117 and 'Subject, Psyche and Agency: The Work of Judith Butler', *Theory, Culture and Society*, 16 (2): 175–93.

A shorter version of chapter 3 appeared as 'Gender and Narrative Identity', *Journal of Political Ideologies*, 4 (3): 315–36.

1

GENDER, SUBJECTIFICATION
AND AGENCY: INTRODUCTORY
REMARKS

From negative to generative paradigm

In the last few years, a cluster of issues pertaining to the question of agency have become the renewed focus of thought in feminist and social theory. The concern with the concept of agency has been initiated, in part, by more general reflections on the changing nature of economic and social structures in late-capitalist societies. The many debates about modernity, postmodernity, reflexive modernization, globalization and detraditionalization address in various ways questions about the changing nature of action in a society which, it is claimed, is becoming increasingly complex, plural and uncertain.

One of the most pronounced effects of these macrostructural tendencies towards detraditionalization is the transformation of the social status of women in the last forty years and the restructuring of gender relations that it has arguably initiated. The effects of these processes of gender restructuring upon the lives of men and women are ambiguous in that they do not straightforwardly reinforce old forms of gender inequality; nor, however, can their detraditionalizing impact be regarded as wholly emancipatory. New forms of autonomy and constraint can be seen to be emerging which can no longer be understood through dichotomies of male domination and female subordination. Instead, inequalities are emerging along generational, class and racial lines where structural divisions amongst women are as significant as divisions between men and women. Feminist theory has registered the ambiguous effects of these social changes through a rethinking of the concepts of gender identity and agency. In so far as these concepts, inherited from first-wave feminism, are premised upon notions of patriarchal domination, they do not explain sufficiently the types of behaviour and action exhibited by men and women in their negotiation of complex social relations. In short, underlying the move away from what are regarded as relatively ahistorical theories of patriarchy and female subordination is an attempt to reconceptualize agency which, in feminist theory, is often formulated as explanations of how gender identity is a durable but not immutable phenomenon.

The conceptualization of gender identity as durable but not immutable has prompted a rethinking of agency in terms of the inherent instability of gender norms and the consequent possibilities for resistance, subversion and the emancipatory remodelling of identity (e.g. Butler 1990, 1993a; Pellegrini 1997; Sedgewick 1994). This book is a contribution to that project of thinking through aspects of the dialectic of stasis and change within gender identity and its implications for a theory of agency. My central claim, however, is that recent theoretical work on identity offers only a partial account of agency because it remains within an essentially negative understanding of subject formation. If, following Michel Foucault, the process of subjectification is understood as a dialectic of freedom and constraint – 'the subject is constituted through practices of subjection, or, in a more autonomous way, through practices of liberation, of liberty' – then it is the negative moment of subjection that has been accorded theoretical privilege in much work on identity construction (Foucault 1988: 50). The predominance of a primarily negative paradigm of identity formation – of subjectification as subjection – comes from the poststructural emphasis on the subject as discursive effect and is a theme common to both Foucauldian constructionism and Lacanian psychoanalysis. The idea of the subject formed through an originary act of constraint has been particularly powerful for feminist theory because it offers a way of analysing the deeply entrenched aspects of gendered behaviour while eschewing reference to a presocial sexual difference. I do not dispute the power of this negative paradigm of subjectification for an examination of the seemingly compulsory nature of the sex–gender system. I question, however, the extent to which it is generalized in much recent theoretical work on identity to become an exhaustive explanation of all aspects of subjectivity and agency. The idea that the individual emerges from constraint does not offer a broad enough understanding of the dynamics of subjectification and, as a consequence, offers an etiolated understanding of agency.

Although it is formulated in diverse ways, the main contention of the negative paradigm is that coherent subjectivity is discursively or symbolically constructed. This idea of discursive construction becomes a form of determinism because of the frequent assumption, albeit implicit, of the essential passivity of the subject. This uni-directional and repressive dynamic is reinforced by the exclusionary logic that is used to invest the subject with levels of self-awareness and autonomy. Following a relational theory of meaning, the assertion of the subject's identity is explained through a logic of the disavowal of difference; the subject maintains a sense of self principally through a denial of the alterity of the other. While this might be a foundational moment in the formation of coherent subjectivity, it does not provide on its own a comprehensive explanation of all possible ways in which the subject may relate to the other or deal with difference. When this exclusionary logic is extended to explain all aspects of subject formation, it results in an attenuated account of agency which leaves unexplored how individuals are endowed with the capabilities for independent reflection and action such that their response, when confronted with difference and paradox, may involve accommodation or adaptation as much as denial. In other words, it leaves unexplained the capabilities of individuals to respond to difference in a less defensive and even, at times, a more creative fashion. Arguably, it is such qualities that are partially characteristic of the responses of women and men to processes of gender restructuring in late-capitalist societies.

This is not to say that the negative paradigm of subjectification does not offer a theory of agency, but it tends to think of

action mainly through the residual categories of resistance to
or dislocation of dominant norms. In part, the predominance
of the cluster of ideas of dislocation, resistance, hybridity and
resignification in work on identity construction stems from the
rejection of unfeasible Marxist notions of revolutionary praxis
that dominated radical theories of change and agency during
the early 1970s (e.g. Foucault 1980: 78–108). Such ideas denote strategies of subversion which have a more tangential
relation to dominant forms than directly oppositional and fully
self-conscious models of revolutionary change. Yet the terms
resistance and dislocation have, in some respects, become
truisms in that they are used to describe any situation where
individual practices do not conform to dominant norms. This
is a tendency evident, for example, in some types of cultural
studies which impute to certain everyday practices a kind of
inherently subversive status (McNay 1996). Yet, if it is ac-
cepted that individual practices never reflect overarching norms
in a straightforward fashion, then this widely deployed notion
of resistance loses analytical purchase. This is not to deny the
efficacy of all forms of resistance, but it is to suggest that a
more precise and varied account of agency is required to explain the differing motivations and ways in which individuals
and groups struggle over, appropriate and transform cultural
meanings and resources. This, in turn, indicates the necessity
of contextualizing agency within power relations in order to
understand how acts deemed as resistant may transcend their
immediate sphere in order to transform collective behaviour
and norms.

   This attempt to sketch out other aspects of subjectification
and agency which have been underelaborated in the negative
paradigm involves trying to integrate the idea of a determining
constraint within a more *generative* theoretical framework. The
symbolic determinism of the negative paradigm is partially
overcome, for example, through a more *dialogical understanding of the temporal* aspects of subject formation. The emphasis
in the negative paradigm on subjection tends to highlight
the retentive dimension of the sedimented effects of power
upon the body. This underplays the protensive or future-
oriented dimension of praxis as the living through of embodied

potentialities, and as the anticipatory aspects inherent within subject formation. Unravelling some of these dialogical relations replaces the stasis of determinist models with a generative logic which yields a more persuasive account of the emergence of agency. The main implication of this generative logic for a theory of agency, which is taken up in this book, is that it yields an understanding of a creative or imaginative substrate to action. It is crucial to conceptualize these creative or productive aspects immanent to agency in order to explain how, when faced with complexity and difference, individuals may respond in unanticipated and innovative ways which may hinder, reinforce or catalyse social change. With regard to issues of gender, a more rounded conception of agency is crucial to explaining both how women have acted autonomously in the past despite constricting social sanctions and also how they may act now in the context of processes of gender restructuring. I also argue that attendant on the conceptualization of a creative dimension to agency are renewed understandings of ideas of autonomy and reflexivity, understood as the critical awareness that arises from a self-conscious relation with the other. These concepts have proved problematic for feminist theorists, in particular, because of their association with a form of masculinist abstraction that privileges a disembedded and disembodied subject. I argue, however, that the converse insistence, made by many feminists, on the ineluctably situated nature of the subject hinders the conceptualization of agency in so far as it necessarily involves a partial transcendence of its material conditions of emergence.

The account of a creative substrate to agency that arises from a generative account of subjectification also results in a slightly altered perspective on certain problems upon which much work on identity has become fixated. Some of these problems appear particularly intractable because of an unhelpful polarization that is an effect of the debate over essentialism which preoccupied feminist and other work on identity during the late 1970s and early 1980s. I do not make the grandiose claim that these very difficult issues are overcome through a reformulated account of subject formation, but rather that they may be reconfigured. The term reconfiguration suggests that by slightly rearranging the relations existing between elements within a given theoretical constellation, insight might be generated into ways of moving beyond certain overplayed dualisms and exegetical clichés. I focus, in particular, on the insights that a generative account of subjectification and agency offers into three clusters of issues that have predominated in much thought on the construction of the subject: the relation between the material and symbolic dimensions of subjectification; the issue of the identity or coherence of the self; and, finally, the relation between the psyche and the social. To enable a more detailed discussion of these issues, I will discuss the negative paradigm of subjectification, as it is formulated in the thought of Foucault and Lacan, and its relation to feminist thought on subjectivity and agency.

The subject in Foucault and Lacan

Much feminist work on gender identity is dominated by the thought of Foucault and Lacan, which exemplifies some of the major features of the negative paradigm of subjectification. Although feminists have considered in detail the shortcomings of their thought, particularly with regard to integrating an account of agency into an understanding of the formation of gender identity, there have, on the whole, been few attempts to locate alternative theoretical sources beyond these two paradigms.

Lacan's thought has had an enormous impact upon feminist psychoanalytical accounts of the formation of gender, principally because his interpretation of Freud through structural linguistics permits an account of the institution of sexual identity that is not biologically reductionist. These aspects of Lacan's work are extensively discussed in feminist literature and, therefore, will only be briefly set out here (e.g. Gallop 1982; Grosz 1990; Ragland-Sullivan 1986). For Lacan, the stable subject is an illusion which obscures the ceaseless disruption of identity by the workings of the unconscious. The imaginary aspect to the formation of the stable subject or 'I' can be discerned in a 'primordial form' in Lacan's account of infant self-identification during the 'mirror stage' where lack is connected to the

anatomical underdevelopment of the infant which is con-
cealed by the illusion of a premature corporeal unity given in
the reflection. The dilemmas of the mirror stage prefigure the
dynamic of the subsequent formation of the subject within
language or the 'field of the Other' (Lacan 1977c: 203). The
formation of the subject within language is crucially linked to
the ambiguous status of the sign itself. Signifiers in themselves
have no absolute meaning for meaning is only the effect of a
negative relation between signifiers (Rose 1982: 32–3). The
subject can only emerge as such within language. At the same
time, however, the unstable nature of language means that, at
the moment of its appearance, the subject is 'petrified' or
reduced to being no more than a signifier. The subject is constituted within the other of language, but language cannot
confer on the subject any absolute guarantee of its meaning.
This play of presence–absence which characterizes the emergence of the 'I' within language is what Lacan calls the 'fading'
of the subject (*aphanisis*): '*aphanisis* is to be situated in a more
radical way at the level at which the subject manifests himself
in this movement of disappearance that I have described as
lethal . . . I have called this movement the *fading* of the subject' (Lacan 1977c: 207–8). The disappearance of the subject
is connected to the movement of the unconscious which eludes
capture within language and which is located beneath the
networks and chains of the signifier in an 'indeterminate
place' (1977c: 208). Thus, despite the persistence of the subject's belief in the wholeness of its identity, the subject is in
fact constituted upon a fundamental lack or division. In terms
of the instauration of gender identity, this lack ensures that
there is no inevitability or stability to the process whereby
women and men assume feminine and masculine identities.
The stabilization of identity is constantly thwarted by the
destabilizing effects of the unconscious upon the symbolic
order of phallocentric meaning.

The difficulty with Lacan's linguistic account of subjectification, it is widely argued, is that the ahistorical and formal nature
of the paradigm forecloses a satisfactory account of agency.
This is most evident in the description of the phallocentric
construction of feminine identity, which is construed in such

univocally negative terms – woman as double lack – that it is difficult to see how it connects to the concrete practices and achievements of women as social agents. The uni-directional account of subject formation as the introjection of the repressive law of the symbolic results in a monolithic account of the phallocentric order which remains essentially unaltered by social and historical variations. Although the destabilizing force of the category of the unconscious points to ways in which the internalization of the law of the symbolic can be resisted, a more substantive account of agency beyond the individualist terms of a libidinal politics is foreclosed. The socio-historical specificity of agency and of particular struggles is denied by being reduced to an effect of an ahistorical and self-identical principle of non-adequation between psyche and society. Indeed, agency is imputed to the pre-reflexive realm of the unconscious, rather than being conceived of as the property of determinate historical praxis. A further difficulty for feminist theory is that the priority that is accorded to the phallus in determining meaning within the symbolic realm means that agency is usually only considered in relation to sexual difference.

Running counter to Lacan's thought, the work of Michel Foucault on the body and power has been one of the most influential sources for the development of constructionist accounts of subject formation. The impact of his work upon feminist theories of gender identity and agency is so well known that it need not be gone into here (Diamond and Quinby 1988; McNay 1992; Ramazonglu 1993). It is a widely rehearsed criticism that Foucault's earlier work on discipline lacks a concept of subjectivity and, therefore, also precludes a theory of agency by reducing individuals to docile bodies. The major part of his oeuvre, from *Psychiatry and Mental Illness* to the first volume of *The History of Sexuality*, exemplifies the negative paradigm of subjectification in that it is devoted to exploring the different ways in which the identity of dominant groups has been maintained through the exclusion and derogation of marginal groups and liminal experiences.

The lack of a substantive category of subjectivity is corrected in Foucault's final work where he sets out the idea of 'technologies of the self' understood as the practices and techniques

through which individuals actively fashion their own identities. This active process of self-formation suggests how the
seemingly inexorable processes of corporeal inculcation, or
'technologies of domination', may be resisted through the self-
conscious stylization of identity like a work of art. Individuals
are regarded as relatively autonomous in so far as the process
of identity formation involves neither passive submission to
external constraints nor willed adoption of dominant norms
(McNay 1992). However, Foucault's idea of the self does not
really offer a satisfactory account of agency. Although the idea
of practices of the self or an 'aesthetics of existence' gestures
towards the autonomous and even creative element inherent
to action, it is asserted rather than elaborated in detail. For
example, the status of the self-fashioning subject who appears
to precede an ethics of the self remains unexplained. The
failure to distinguish more precisely between practices of the
self that are imposed on individuals through cultural sanctions
and those that are more freely adopted also means that the
idea of agency ultimately has voluntarist connotations. The
lack of detail in Foucault's consideration of how the dialectic
of freedom and constraint is realized in the process of subject
formation results, ultimately, in his thought vacillating between
the moments of determinism and voluntarism. The insights in
the work on discipline are not fully integrated with the later
work on the self and so Foucault can only offer the overdeterminist view of the subject subsumed by the operations of
power upon the body or the solipsistic outlook of an aesthetics
of existence.

While Foucault's work does not foreclose an account of
agency in so stark a manner as the Lacanian reification of the
phallocentric order, it is seriously limited by its conceptual
underdevelopment. Despite the lack of a detailed account of
agency, much feminist and other constructionist theory of identity tends to remain within a Foucauldian paradigm. This is
evident, for example, in the work of Susan Hekman (1995),
who criticizes the work of thinkers such as Teresa De Lauretis
(1987) and Paul Smith (1988) for deploying 'dialectical' notions
of subjectification which fail to break from a dualist model
where a Cartesian concept of agency is grafted mechanistically

onto a pre-given subject. Against this dichotomous concept of the constituting–constituted subject, Hekman argues that Foucault's idea of the construction of the self as a 'work of art' exemplifies an alternative, monological and active sense of agency. However, given the elliptical nature and voluntarist implications of Foucault's account of self-formation, it is hard to see how it breaks substantively from other dualist conceptions. In order, therefore, to understand the creative elements of action that are so suggestive in Foucault's idea of an aesthetics of existence, it would seem necessary, if not to move beyond the negative paradigm, at least to enlarge it with a more generative account of subject formation and agency.

Agency in feminism

On the most general level, a revised understanding of agency has long been the explicit or implicit concern of feminist research devoted to the uncovering of the marginalized experiences of women. These experiences attest to the capacity for autonomous action in the face of often overwhelming cultural sanctions and structural inequalities. This unifying impulse notwithstanding, the concept of agency has been theorized in ways which mirror bifurcations in feminist thought. Echoing conceptual problems in mainstream social theory, feminist thought could be said to be divided between the relatively unmediated notions of agency and practice characteristic of microsociological and relational theories, on the one hand, and the discursively determinist accounts of poststructural feminist theory, on the other.

Within sociology, the exploration of female agency has been conducted mainly at the level of interpretative microsociology, particularly feminist ethnomethodology. A problem with this work on the submerged practices of women and other marginal groups is that it can too easily slip into a celebration of these experiences as somehow primary or authentic. This is evident, for example, in the work of feminist standpoint theorists, such as Dorothy Smith (1987), who accord an epistemological privilege to women's dual perspective on social reality.

It is also evident in certain types of women's history which, as Joan Scott has shown, rely heavily on an appeal to experience as an originary point of explanation (Scott 1991: 786–7). The rapid transformation in women's social status in late-capitalist society combined with the black feminist critique of feminism and the poststructural problematization of identity have all triggered the recognition that these celebratory accounts of agency which rely on a dualism of male dominance and female subordination do not capture adequately the complexities of agency in an era of transformation in gender relations. As Patricia Mann puts it, 'it is necessary to expand the vocabulary of political actions in order to make sense of individual agency in moments of discursive uncertainty and political change' (Mann 1994: 17).

Within feminist theory, one of the main alternative paradigms to poststructural ideas on the construction of gender are the various relational accounts of subjectification offered in object relations theory and Habermasian feminism. Although this stream of thought is not the main focus of this book, some of the limitations of their tacitly naturalized accounts of agency should briefly be considered. Against the poststructural emphasis on the discursive construction of subjectivity, relational accounts tend to emphasize the constitutive role of the intersubjective dynamic in the establishment of gender identity. In the object relations approach of Nancy Chodorow and Carol Gilligan, the intersubjective dynamic is paradigmatically expressed in the mother–child dyad which, as has been widely pointed out, has the effect of naturalizing the process through which gender identity is assumed (Held 1987; Soper 1990). The idea of agency that can be extrapolated from such an account of subjectification is curtailed by the reliance upon an inevitable sexual difference. Moreover, within that limited paradigm, it is only the role of the mother that is theorized. Such tacitly maternal accounts of agency are insufficient to explain changes within patterns of gendered behaviour which are, to a large extent, catalysed by tensions arising from the expansion of women's role beyond that of mothering.

An alternative strand within relational theories of gender is the work of Habermasian feminists such as Selya Benhabib

(1992) and Jodi Dean (1996) on the communicative dimensions to subject formation. This work attempts to overcome the naturalizing tendencies of object relations theory by socializing the relational dyamic. Nonetheless, the concept of agency that emerges is limited because its understanding of intersubjective relations is underpinned by an implicitly domesticated concept of difference. Habermas's distinction between system and lifeworld forecloses an understanding of the structural aspects to gender reproduction by confining gender identity to the normatively oriented rationality of the lifeworld (Fraser 1989). This foreclosure of an examination of structural elements in the reproduction of gender norms means that subjectification occurs through intersubjectivity understood primarily as *immediate* interpersonal relations (the *concrete other*). This model fails to take on board fully the implications of a notion of *extended* intersubjective relations for gender identity, that is, relations that are mediated through impersonal symbolic and material structures. The mediation of gender forms through such structural mechanisms renders the levels of reflexivity presumed in the intersubjective dynamic more problematic than is often recognized in the Habermasian model. The linguistic monism of this model tends to gloss over the blockages, both psychic and social, that may hinder transparency of the self both to itself and others (e.g. Coole 1996; Whitebook 1995). This can be seen as symptomatic of an increasing stress on the management of the self in late modernity which, as Ian Craib argues in *The Importance of Disappointment*, leads to the rise of anodyne notions of subjectivity based on respect and equality which suppress the irrational and often negative contents of identity such as jealousy, possessiveness, devotion, sacrifice, rage and brutality (Craib 1994: 178). This results in a sanitized view of gender subjectivity and agency which, in so far as it elevates the mothering role, is not that dissimilar to feminist object relations theory. In sum, although relational accounts of subjectification offer notions of agency beyond the negative paradigm, they are undercut either by being framed in the naturalized terms of the maternal function or, as a result of the requirement of reflexive and reciprocal communicative structures, by being predicated on untenable levels of self-transparency.

Counterposed to such relational theories are the ideas of the discursive construction of the subject offered in post-Foucauldian theory. Within feminist thought, the proliferation of recent work on the theme of embodiment represents, in part, an attempt to elaborate in more detail Foucault's original insight into how processes of bodily inscription can result in the formation of the autonomous subject. Feminist theorists, in particular, have focused on this question of embodiment because it is crucial for analysing how the effects of dominant, sexualized notions of 'Woman' upon the dispositions and practices of women may be oppressive but are not completely determining. In other words, despite the imperatives of the sex–gender system ('compulsory heterosexuality'), women (and men) do not remain prisoners of their sex as some feminist thought seems to imply (e.g. Bartky 1988). Feminists have argued that the category of embodiment replaces dichotomous formulations of the relation between mind and body with monistic and more dialogical conceptions. The emphasis on praxeological or lived aspects to corporeal being suggests a more fluid relation between body and subjectivity than is available in dualist concepts. This monistic approach expresses a revised understanding of gender identity as not simply imposed through patriarchal structures, but as a set of norms that are lived and transformed in the embodied practices of men and women. The instability of gender norms arises from the inherent historicity of social practices. There is a shift, therefore, from understanding the sex–gender system as an atemporal structure towards an alternative concept of a series of interconnected regimes whose relations are historically variable and dynamic. This idea of gender as a historical matrix, rather than a static structure, is regarded as offering a more substantive account of agency.

Despite the insights generated by this work on embodied identity, theoretical difficulties arise which reflect certain limitations of remaining within a negative paradigm of subjectification. It is these limitations with regard to introducing a theory of agency into gender discourse which will now be considered to enable comparison with the approach suggested by a generative account of subject formation and agency.

The material and the symbolic

With regard to the relation between the material and symbolic, one of the limitations of recent feminist work on embodiment is that it remains largely within a symbolic, or more
narrowly a linguistic, conception of the construction of corporeal identity. Following the linguistic turn initiated by
poststructural thought, difference is understood principally as
instability within meaning systems and not, in more sociological terms, as the differentiated power relations constitutive
of the social realm. The primacy accorded to linguistic accounts of subject formation results in what Stuart Hall has
called a 'reduction upwards' in which the only issue considered is positionality in relation to sexual difference in language (Hall 1997: 33). An effect of the primacy accorded to
symbolic accounts of subjectification is that material dynamics
in the process of identity formation are not considered. For
example, the issue of the social reproduction of gender inequalities is often reduced to the narrower question of the symbolic
construction of sexual identity. Constructionist thought frequently alludes to material dimensions of power, but an understanding of the way in which the symbolic dimensions of
subjectification are refracted through these structures is often
not developed sufficiently. Whilst all social practices are to
some degree linguistically mediated, they are not necessarily
linguistic in nature; patterns of employment discrimination or
economic exclusion are deeply sedimented, complex and reproduced in ways that the linguistic model does not adequately
capture.

The importance of understanding the intertwinement of
both material and symbolic practices in the construction
of the gendered subject is not new. It was a major concern of
first-wave feminist work, which tried to capture these complex
interrelations through ideas of patriarchy (e.g. the debate over
dual systems theory or the domestic labour debate) or the sex–
gender system (Hartmann 1981; Mitchell 1974; Rubin 1975).
For various well-rehearsed reasons, this work has been criticized for being too rigid and essentializing in its analysis of

gender subordination (Connell 1987: 41–66). Yet, as overstated as this early work may have been, it attempted to connect the psychosexual dimensions of gender identity to a range of social and economic imperatives in a way that contemporary feminism has neglected because of its bifurcation into materialist and symbolic forms of analysis. From a materialist perspective, Nancy Fraser (1997) has argued that certain Foucauldian-influenced work on the construction of identity has led to an overemphasis within feminist thought on a symbolic or cultural politics of recognition that disregards underlying issues of economic disadvantage. For Fraser, it is crucial to recognize that gender is simultaneously constructed along symbolic and material dimensions in order to undo the false antithesis between a politics of recognition and one of redistribution. Other materialist feminists have criticized the emphasis on marginal sexualities within feminist work on embodiment because it results in an under-theorization of heterosexuality (Hull 1997). The concentration within feminist work on sexuality upon the emergence of non-heterosexual or 'excentric' sexualities means that the norm of heterosexuality is deemed, explicitly or implicitly, to be relatively unproblematic. In fact, arguably, processes of gender restructuring are far more complex than the distinction between the normal and the excluded allows. In reaction to this focusing on 'excentric' sexualities, there has emerged a 'theorizing heterosexuality' stream within materialist feminism which focuses on the economic and institutional dimensions of gender inequality, rather than issues connected to the psychosexual formation of the subject (Richardson 1996; VanEvery 1995). This sociological work claims that there is little evidence to suggest that, despite the increased opportunities for women in education and the labour market, the gender division of labour within the household is altering significantly (Franks 1999). The persistence of discriminatory practices at work, continued pay disparities between men and women and phenomena such as the 'feminization of poverty' reinforce the view that if change is occurring it is extremely gradual. In this view, the restructuring of gender relations does not involve a steady increase in women's autonomy, but involves a shift to new forms of inequality,

exemplified in Walby's idea of the move from private to public patriarchy (Walby 1990).

In short, materialist feminists have a more cautious view
of the potential for a transformation of gender relations than
certain work within symbolic feminism. From a materialist perspective, a linguistic understanding of subject formation reduces
gender to the issue of sexuality, leads to an overestimation of
the instability of symbolic structures and to an exaggeration of
the emancipatory effects of alternative libidinal practices. The
economic, political and social dimensions of gender inequality
are all subsumed under what Gayatri Spivak has called the
'fetish of identity' (Spivak 1993). There is much force to these
criticisms, but the weakness of materialist feminism is that the
emphasis placed on economic, political and social structures of
exclusion can result in a determinist analysis which lacks an
understanding of how these structural forces are worked through
at the level of subject formation and agency. For example, in
an attempt to map the complex shifts within gender relations,
Sylvia Walby (1990) disaggregrates the concept of patriarchy
into seven regimes which, although characterized by their
respective internal logics, are closely interrelated. Yet, what her
analysis lacks is any mediatory category, such as agency, through
which it is possible to understand how these structural relations operate at the level of daily life. Thus Walby finishes
with a systemic account of gender hierarchy which disregards
the impact of these macrostructural shifts upon the individual
who moves between and negotiates different sets of power
relations.

The relationship between symbolic and material practices
can begin to be understood more adequately with the shift
from a determinist to a generative account of subjectification
and agency. When the formation of subjectivity is understood
not in one-sided terms as an exogenously imposed effect but
as result of a lived relation between embodied potentiality and
material relations, then an active concept of agency emerges.
Understanding agency partly as the capacity to manage actively the often discontinuous, overlapping or conflicting relations of power provides a point from which to examine the
connection between the symbolic and material relations that

are constitutive of a differentiated social order. This idea of difference, not just as indeterminacy within systems of meaning, but as social complexity, is often alluded to in constructionist work but is undercut by its symbolic determinism which pre-empts a substantive category of agency through which the idea of differentiation can be developed.

Personal identity

The second cluster of issues with which this book is concerned relate to the theme of personal identity or the coherence of the self. Poststructural theory has criticized the idea of the identity of the self by deconstructing its unity and revealing it to be an illusory effect emerging from the uneasy suturing of incommensurable discursive positions. A difficulty that emerges from this emphasis on the dispersed nature of identity is that subjectivity becomes a free-floating and atemporal entity which lacks historical depth or *durée*. An unqualified constructivism or nominalism emerges where subjectivity is regarded as being relatively amenable to processes of reconstruction. The problem of nominalism is compounded by the relational account of meaning that underpins the negative paradigm of subjectification which is often generalized to mean that, if identities have no positive content, then they may be rebuilt in a potentially endless variety of other modes (Bauman 1995; Kellner 1992). Such formal accounts lack a sense of the historical and social embeddedness of subject formations and the ways in which some types of identity are more durable than others. This lack of depth to the contingent subject of poststructural thought fails to recognize that the site occupied by the historical subject is characterized by the conjuncture of heterogeneous temporal dimensions or a 'contemporaneity of the non-contemporaneous' (Kosselleck 1985: xiii). In short, ideas of temporal differentiation and lag throw into question the extent to which subjective formations are open to processes of refashioning.

Feminist work on embodiment has attempted to overcome the nominalist tendencies of an unqualified constructivism

partially through an emphasis on the repetitive, lived aspects
of sexual identity which suggests ideas of entrenchment and
resistance. Such ideas are not captured adequately, for example, in the underdetermined relation of contingency posited
by the sex–gender distinction (McNay 1992: 22–3). Gender
identities are not free-floating: they involve deep-rooted investments on the part of individuals and historically sedimented
practices which severely limit their transferability and transformability. Although subject formations receive their shape
from prevailing social conditions, certain predispositions and
tendencies may still continue to effect embodied practices long
after their original conditions of emergence have been surpassed. This durability partly suggests that a coherent sense of
self is not just an illusion but fundamental to the way in which
the subject interprets itself in time. Although feminist work
on embodiment goes some way to overcoming the unqualified
notion of the contingent nature of subjectivity, it tends to
leave the coherence of the self unthought. Indeed, in response
to pervasive processes of corporeal inculcation, feminist theory
has often explicitly or implicitly dismissed the category of
identity as inherently exclusionary. Thus, the emancipatory
force of a libidinal politics is seen to reside in a refusal of all
identifications. As well as resting on a problematic fetishization
of the inchoate, the wholesale rejection of identity initiates a
chain of dualisms of identity versus non-identity, the normal
and the excluded, the marginal and the central which hinder
the development of an active account of agency in feminist
thought. It also seems to ignore the point that the 'excluded'
and the 'marginal' are kinds of identity. Concepts such as
reflexivity and autonomy which are central to an account of
action are rejected because of their association with 'identarian'
thought. In the final analysis, it becomes difficult to conceptualize agency beyond the apodictic radicality with which the idea
of indeterminacy is invested.

A generative paradigm of subjectification and agency helps
to unpack such overplayed oppositions by conceptualizing
the coherence of the self as a simultaneity of identity and
non-identity. Through a temporalization of the process of
subjectification, the generative model suggests that the self has

unity but it is the dynamic unity of progress in time. In other words, the identity of the self is maintained only through a ceaseless incorporation of the non-identical understood as temporal flux. The idea of active configuration that underlies the idea of the formation of coherent selfhood offers a renewed way of thinking about stasis and change within identity be-yond the dichotomous logic of the essentialism debate and also delineates the imaginative or creative dimensions immanent to agency. Thinking through aspects to the maintenance of a coherent sense of personal identity helps explain the discon-tinuous nature of change in gender relations in terms of the investments individuals may have in certain self-conceptions that render them resistant to transformation.

Psyche and society

The final set of problems associated with the negative para-digm which persist within certain feminist theories on gender are those that relate to understanding the link between the psychic and social dimensions of subject formation. Construc-tionist and psychoanalytic accounts of subjectivity are often seen as mutually exclusive because of the claimed functional-ism of the former and the ahistorical nature of the latter. Yet the opposition needs to be overcome if agency is to be under-stood both as historically variable and as driven by deep-seated and often opaque motivations. Recent feminist theory has attempted to overcome the opposition between psyche and society, replacing it with the idea of a relation of mutual non-inherence or supervenience where neither side is reducible to the other (Brennan 1993; Butler 1997b). For example, in *Volatile Bodies*, Elizabeth Grosz (1994a) considers the process of subject formation through the image of the Möbius strip which replaces dualist understandings of the relation between psychical interior and corporeal exterior (mind–body, inside–outside) with the idea of torsion of one into another. The idea of a reciprocal determination blocks the assertion of the causal primacy of psyche over society or vice versa; it is only by being projected out into the social that the contents of the psyche receive their form. From the idea of mutual inherence emerges a concept of the body as a transitional entity where corporeal identity is regarded as unfinished and as relatively amenable to transformation.

The linking together of the psychic and the social dimensions of subject formation in the idea of inherence is extremely suggestive but the potential of the relation has not been fully realized. This is because of the tendency of feminist psychoanalytic theory to remain within the discursive determinism of the negative paradigm which, at the limit, makes it difficult to transcend the society–psyche dualism where one side ultimately retains causal priority over the other. Moreover, psychoanalytic theory tends to displace the causes of agency onto the category of the unconscious and its destabilizing effects within the symbolic order. The problem arises that agency is then conflated with a presocial force whose ahistorical, self-identical dynamic forecloses a recognition of the historically determinate nature of action. It also results in the problematic attribution of an inherently radical status to the pre-conscious realm. At the same time, subjectification is construed in the essentially passive terms of the introjection of phallocentric meaning where the symbolic order is both unchanging and all-powerful. The essentially ahistorical understanding of the symbolic order precludes an account of agency in terms of the ability to behave in an autonomous or unexpected fashion because accommodation to the Law of the Father is seen as an inevitable cost of subjectification.

The implications of the idea of an inherence between psyche and society can be more fully explained with the move from a determinist to a generative paradigm of subject formation. To develop the idea of inherence, it is necessary, on the one side, to formulate an explicitly sociocentric understanding of the symbolic realm understood as a differentiated and contested order of meaning rather than as the frozen domain of phallocentric signification. On the other side, the category of the unconscious needs to be conceptualized in more substantive terms, not purely as lack, but as an originary capacity for figuration. The mutual inherence of the symbolic and the psyche can then be explained in terms of a generative dynamic of 'leaning on' or drawing out. One of the main implications of this idea of inherence is that it yields a concept of agency more easily than the negative paradigm where the idea of agency is either reducible to the subversions of the unconscious or undercut as an illusion of the symbolic order. Instead, agency is configured as a capacity to institute new or unanticipated modes of behaviour, the ontological grounds of which lie in the originary capacity for figuration but which are not reducible to it because of the dynamic nature of the social order.

Agency in social theory

The conceptualization of the process of subjectification in more generative terms offers an account of the creative or imaginative aspects to action which is essential to understanding various modalities of agency. In order to develop this argument I draw on the work of European social theorists for whom the theme of the creativity of action has been a central concern. This is not to imply that these social theorists have succeeded in developing a more substantive account of agency where feminist theorists have failed. The divisions within feminist thought are, of course, reflective of wider difficulties in social theory connected to the elaboration of a theory of agency beyond the constraints of interpretative and determinist approaches (Maffesoli 1996: 7). Nor does it imply that the encounter staged here between feminism and social theory is one-way. In elaborating theories of gender identity, feminist theorists have engaged extensively with social theory, but social theorists, on the whole, have failed to take on board the implications of feminist and other work on gender. Indeed, part of the argument made here is that thought on subjectification and agency within social theory is weakened by the lack of consideration given to issues of gender identity. For example, following on from Etzioni's (1968) influential reformulation of agency in the idea of the active society, recent debates in social theory on the effects of globalization, detraditionalization and reflexive modernization can be seen to be explicitly or implicitly deploying a more nuanced model of action which operates outside the aporia of determinism and voluntarism (Sztompka 1994: 36–8). Thinkers such as Anthony Giddens, Scott Lash and Ulrich Beck claim that processes of societal detraditionalization, triggered by the globalization of capitalist structures, have resulted in the attenuation of conventional gender norms. Although the outcome of this attenuation is increased levels of personal insecurity or ontological anxiety – such as the 'normal chaos of love' – a potentially emancipatory restructuring of gender relations is simultaneously made possible. While some of these thinkers of identity transformation deploy the caveat that they are pointing out the utopian potential inherent in processes of social disorganization, certain of their claims with regard to shifts in gender norms are not formulated with sufficient caution. The speculative nature of some arguments about the transformability of identity arises from the fact that these thinkers often work with a primarily symbolic account of identity which tends to disregard the more entrenched, embodied and psychic aspects of identity and the extent to which the somatization of gender norms renders them resistant to social change. As a result, certain of these theorists tend to overemphasize the mutability of identity, positing a short-circuit between shifts in overarching gender norms and in individual practices. While self-conscious creativity may be a characteristic of certain types of action, it should not be understood as a generalizable characteristic of agency in 'post-conventional' societies. The uneven and conflictual nature of change within gender relations suggests that it is a more complex and evanescent feature of action.

It follows that the attempt to reconfigure agency in terms of the creativity of action is not to fall into a celebration of praxis *per se*. The uncovering of a creative or imaginative substrate to action does not amount to a valorization of agency; it is necessary, however, to explain how action transcends its material context. A creative dimension to action is the condition of possibility of certain types of autonomous agency understood as the ability to act in an unexpected fashion or to institute new and unanticipated modes of behaviour. Such forms of agency underlie certain transformations within gender relations. However, the social theoretical concern with power relations serves as a reminder that any theory of agency must be placed in the context of structural, institutional or intersubjective constraints.

The creativity of action has been a particularly prevalent theme within a certain strand of continental theory and it is upon this that I draw to develop arguments about sub-jectification and agency. In different ways, Pierre Bourdieu, Paul Ricoeur and Cornelius Castoriadis attempt to escape from a determinist or instrumental model of agency by reconstruing subjectification as a generative process. By emphasizing the latent element of creativity within action, each thinker offers a more dynamic model of social reproduction which, to a degree, resonates with the concern of feminist theory to under-stand gender formations as durable but not immutable. In Bourdieu and Ricoeur, this more creative notion of agency is formulated through a temporalization of the autonomy–constraint dialectic that is constitutive of the subject and, in particular, through the anticipatory dimensions of action. Bourdieu develops the temporalized account of agency in the context of the spatial dimensions of power, that is, through the ideas of corporeal dispositions (habitus) and social structure (the *field*). Ricoeur elaborates the temporal dialectic in terms of the *narrative* structure of self-identity. Castoriadis derives an explanation of agency from an account of its ontological foundations in the *radical imaginary*, understood as an originary capacity for figuration. Castoriadis further opens the theoretical space for agency by replacing the idea of the symbolic as the realm of instituted meaning with the historical category of the *social imaginary* characterized in terms of a generative dynamic between instituting and instituted meaning.

The issues of gender and sexuality are not central concerns for any of the thinkers considered and, as a result, there are crucial omissions in their understanding of aspects of subjectification. For example, in the work of Castoriadis and Ricoeur, the question of power structures and unequal social relations is not as directly addressed as it is in the thought of Bourdieu. Thus while their work provides interesting insights into the ontological grounds of identity, feminist work on gen-der shows more clearly how these ideas may be generalized to explain the construction of hierarchical social relations. In contrast, while Bourdieu gestures towards the centrality of gender in symbolic and material oppressions, the residual classism of his perspective prevents the development of this insight. Implicitly, the question of gender is confined to the issue of symbolic violence and its implication within the construction of material inequalities is not adequately examined. In this respect, feminist work demonstrating the centrality of gender regimes to the structuring of social formations highlights significant shortcomings in these social theoretical conceptions of power. Thus, by using the insights offered by each set of theories to interrogate limitations in the other, I hope to show how a reconfigured account of subjectification and agency might help explain shifts within contemporary gender relations.

A possible objection to Castoriadis's presentation of the radical imaginary as the ontological ground of agency and to Ricoeur's ontologization of narrative is that they push conceptions of identity back into a problematic essentialism. A tangential concern of this book is to begin to unravel some of the false conceptual antitheses that are the effect of the debate over essentialism. While, at the time, the debate served to clarify certain issues, the ideas of essentialism and anti-essentialism are really too diffuse to be of much analytical use in thinking about subject formation. In any consideration of identity, ontological claims need to be deployed carefully, but need not necessarily be regarded as essentialist. Accordingly, while the work of Ricoeur and Castoriadis rests on ontological claims about the nature of identity, these are not essentialist in that they do not impute a fixity to the content of identity. For Castoriadis, the radical flux of the imaginary constitutes the condition of possibility from which a myriad of social forms may arise. Similarly, Ricoeur's ontological conception of narrative refers to the inherent temporality of human existence but, beyond that, does not imply an immutable core to identity. If changes within relations between men and women are to be understood, then the process of gender subjectification has to be understood as durable but not unchanging. The ontological claim of poststructural theory that identity is socially constructed does not go very far in distinguishing the different levels at which subject formation operates or in explaining the various modalities through which agency is expressed. The work of the thinkers considered here takes the constructionist perspective further by suggesting that there are necessary aspects to the construction of subjectivity without conferring upon them an immutability. This, in turn, suggests a more nuanced account of agency and change where transformation is conceptualized as non-synchronous and unevenly dispersed across social practices. This goes some way to moving beyond the dichotomous formulations around which work on identity revolves.

The structure and argument of the subsequent chapters is as follows:

Embodiment and power

As we have seen, much feminist work on the construction of identity has centred on the idea of embodiment, which yields a conception of gender as a lived set of embodied potentialities, rather than as an externally imposed set of constraining norms. The temporalization inherent in the idea of embodiment offers a more substantive account of the emergence of agency from the process of bodily inscription. This work is limited, however, by considering embodiment only in relation to the symbolic formation of sexual identity and thus neglecting material and social dimensions to the construction of gender norms. Pierre Bourdieu's work on embodiment through the concepts of habitus and the *field* resonates strongly with this recent feminist theory, but takes it further in understanding the effects of the intersection of symbolic and material dimensions of power upon the body. Habitus expresses the idea that bodily identity is not natural, but involves the inscription of dominant social norms or the 'cultural arbitrary' upon the body. For Bourdieu, the temporality inherent to the concept of habitus denotes not just the processes through which norms are inculcated upon the body, but also the moment of praxis or living through of these norms by the individual. In other words, habitus is defined, not as a determining principle, but as a generative structure. The temporalization of the idea of habitus introduces a praxeological element into the idea of embodiment such that the dialectic of freedom and constraint in subjectification permits the emergence of a concept of agency understood through the idea of 'regulated liberties'. In conjunction with the concept of the field, this idea of agency provides a perspective from which to think the links between symbolic and material dimensions of power. The Weberian notion of the differentiation and autonomization of realms of social action expressed in the idea of the field provides a way of understanding how processes of corporeal inculcation, although primarily psychosexual, can be overlaid, dislocated and transformed by the logic of other fields.

Despite the insights generated by Bourdieu's theoretical framework, in his only extended consideration of sexual difference, an essay on masculine domination, he offers a rather monolithic account of the realization of gender relations in contemporary society. This essay reinforces the view of his critics, amongst them Judith Butler, who claim that the idea of habitus is simply a sophisticated reformulation of a materialist determinism and, therefore, does not offer a theory of agency but simply one of social reproduction. In examining the underlying differences between Butler's and Bourdieu's conceptions of the links between the material and symbolic aspects of power, I argue that Butler fails to take account of the refractory effects which the concept of the field has upon any uni-directional form of material determinism such as a base–superstructure model. This is undoubtedly a difficulty with Bourdieu's essay on masculine domination, namely that he fails to bring the destabilizing implications of the concept of the field to bear upon the notion of the habitus as he does convincingly elsewhere in his work. But, in general, the concept of the field circumvents the tendency to reduce an understanding of gender to sexuality.

The concept of the field also suggests a revised understanding of the reflexive dimension of agency as a form of distantiation. Arguably, it is the increasing movement of women into social fields which have previously been confined to men that is crucial to an understanding of the decline of traditional gender norms. Finally, the concept of the field permits the conceptualization of differentiation within the construction of gender identity, replacing dualisms of the public and private, workplace and domesticity, the central and the marginal with a more complex logic that mirrors the expansion and uncertainty of women's social experience. This, in turn, offers a way of thinking of possible transformations within gender identity as uneven and non-synchronous phenomena.

Narrative and the self

A gap in constructionist accounts of subjectification is that, while suggesting that identity is composed of a multiplicity of subject positions, the coherence of the self is not really explained beyond vague and top-heavy ideas of ideological fixation. This lacuna arises partly because poststructural work on the subject is not adequately situated temporally, so that the coherence of the subject is viewed, in one-dimensional terms, as the externally imposed effect of power. The neglect to think the coherence of the self has reinforced a broader impasse in theory on identity which seems to be stranded in an opposition between so-called essentialist conceptions, on the one hand, and a post-Nietzschean constructivism, on the other. Paul Ricoeur's work on narrative considers the process of subjectification in terms of a dialogical conception of temporality – a dialectic of retention–protention – in order to evoke a more active sense of agency. The coherence of the self is not conceived as an exogenously imposed effect, but as the result of an active process of configuration whereby individuals attempt to make sense of the temporality of existence. Narrative is the privileged medium of this process of self-formation. The process of active appropriation immanent in the construction of narrative identity suggests a more autonomous model of agency than is offered in the negative paradigm.

The temporalized understanding of the self that the idea of narrative captures – that is, the self has unity but it is the dynamic unity of change through time – also goes some way to overcoming oppositions around which much thought on identity tends to revolve, notably the dualism of essential (stasis) versus constructed (change) concepts of identity and that of authentic experience versus ideological distortion. Along with mitigating these dualisms, it also signals a revised approach to the often overstated rejection of the category of identity and consequent endorsement of a politics of non-identity that is prevalent in certain types of feminist and poststructural theory. Ricoeur's idea that narrative identity revolves around the mediation of two irreducible temporal dimensions – *idem* (sameness) and *ipse* (constancy through change) – offers a temporal framework in which to understand the inseparability of the identical from the non-identical in the process of self-formation. The notion of selfhood implied in ipseity is a reminder that an analysis of the complexities of contemporary gender identity cannot be reduced to an account of embodied identity (idem) or sexuality. Moreover, the mediation of the symbolic dimensions of identity through the varying temporal regimes of different social practices offers an account of change within gender as uneven and non-synchronous.

Radical and social imaginaries

Perhaps one of the most vexed issues in thinking through the social construction of identity is the question of the relation between the psyche and society. Yet, it is the interface of these two realms which is indispensable to a feminist understanding of the way in which gender identities operate. An examination of the psychic dimensions of identity sheds light on both the depth of investments in norms of masculinity and femininity and the difficulties men and women have in sustaining these identifications. I argue that the work of the psychoanalyst Cornelius Castoriadis on the ideas of the *radical* and the *social imaginary* presents a revised understanding of the inherence of the psychic within the social and this suggests a fuller understanding of agency than is available in the negative paradigm of subjectification. A fundamental insight of Castoriadis's work is that identity is formed not around a lack, but around an originary capacity for figuration – the radical imaginary. This reformulates the relation between the psyche and the social as one of inherence rather than determination or introjection of one side by the other. The representative flux of the radical imaginary is realised through the social imaginary understood as the realm where societies represent themselves through the generative dynamic of the *instituting–instituted*. The capacity for self-alteration (instituting) or the creation of the new is in perpetual conflict with society's attempt to figure itself as always-already given (instituted), that is, to deny that social order is anything but inevitable.

The ideas of the radical and social imaginaries offer a more differentiated, temporally open notion of the symbolic order as traversed by various vectors of power than the primarily linguistic conceptions that dominate in Lacanian accounts. By conceiving of the symbolic as composed of more than phallocentric meaning, the concept of the social imaginary bypasses the inexorable negativity that is accorded to the process of feminine subjectification. In short, Castoriadis's work offers a sociocentric reformulation of certain psychoanalytic concepts which permits a fuller conceptualization of autonomous agency. For example, if the subjection of women is to be explained through Oedipus, then it must be understood not as a universal feature of the psyche but as a psychological correlate of familial structures in Western societies.

Castoriadis's thought echoes, in a psychoanalytic mode, the thematization of the imaginative and creative elements inherent to action in the work of Bourdieu and Ricoeur. The unconscious as radical flux has the same disruptive tendencies as the Lacanian notion. However, for Castoriadis, although agency arises from the dislocation between the psyche and social, it cannot be reduced to this dissonance. Dissonance between the unconscious and the social realm is the condition of possibility of all identity, but it does not explain the process of active appropriation that is required to explain certain types of action that result in the emergence of new social forms. Castoriadis's work on the inherence of the social and the psychic suggests a view of the agent who actively participates in the world of contested meanings, rather than being the passive bearer of seemingly exogenous and inexorable norms. From the perspective of understanding gender identity, it counters

the Lacanian reification of the phallocentric order by suggesting that the construction of masculine and feminine identities
constitutes only one of many axes of power along which subject formation occurs. Instabilities and changes within gender
relations, then, do not need to be explained always through
reference to a self-identical principle of non-adequation between psyche and society. Rather they can be understood as
arising from the clash of non-congruent power relations that
are mediated through the social imaginary. In other words, a
historically nuanced and dynamic notion of agency is suggested.

2

BODY, POSITION, POWER: BOURDIEU AND BUTLER ON AGENCY

Introduction

Within feminist theory, a prominent thematization of the concept of agency has been through the idea of embodiment which
yields a more open conception of gender identity as a lived set
of embodied potentialities, rather than as an externally imposed
set of constraining norms. The temporalization inherent in the
idea of embodiment offers a more substantive account of the
emergence of agency from a process of corporeal constraint.
Despite the significant insights of this work, the notion of
agency that it puts forward is limited by considering subjectification mainly in terms of a uni-directional process of symbolic
inscription, an idea that is, ultimately, derived from Foucault's
work. A one-sided notion of temporality as retention – as the
sedimentation of disciplinary effects upon the body – is not
counterbalanced sufficiently by a consideration of the protensive
dimension of the living through of embodied norms in praxis.
Ultimately, this imbalance forecloses a substantive account of
agency. The idea of agency is further circumscribed by failing to
consider how the symbolic investment of the body is overlaid and
altered by social and material relations. In other words, gender
is reduced to sexual identity and agency is understood either as
an abstract structural potential or in narrowly libidinal terms.
   Drawing on the work of Pierre Bourdieu, I argue that a
more generative account of the process of subjectification goes

some way to overcoming these difficulties in thinking about agency. Bourdieu's understanding of habitus as a generative rather than a determining structure is expressed in a dialogical temporality denoting both the ways in which norms are inculcated upon the body and also the moment of praxis or living through of these norms. His insistence on the inseparability of habitus from the field suggests a way of considering how the symbolic dimensions of subjectivity connect to overarching social relations. Against claims made in certain theories of detraditionalization, the principle of differentiation encapsulated in the concept of the field suggests that reflexive agency is not a universal feature of late-capitalist societies but rather a discontinuous phenomenon. This, in turn, offers a framework in which to understand the uneven effects of processes of gender restructuring beyond dualisms of the public versus the private or the dominant versus the excluded. Bourdieu's work is not without difficulties, not least in its failure to consider sufficiently the implications of the idea of the field for the gendered habitus. Nonetheless, it indicates ways in which it is possible to think gender and agency beyond the negative paradigm of subjectification.

Embodiment and agency

Much feminist work on gender identity has focused on the idea of embodiment whose dynamic, mediatory connotations are held to partially overcome the dualisms of mind and body, determinism and practice and the material and non-material. The idea denotes a conception of gender identity as a lived set of embodied potentialities rather than as an externally imposed set of constraining norms (e.g. Braidotti 1994; Butler 1993a; Diprose 1994; Grosz 1994a). The antinomic moments of determinism and voluntarism are mediated by replacing Cartesian dualisms with the idea of a mutual inherence or univocity of mind and body. Above all, the feminist thematization of the idea of embodiment emphasizes the unfinished and unstable elements of corporeal existence. As the point of overlap between the physical, the symbolic and the sociological, the body is a dynamic, mutable frontier. It is the threshold through which the subject's lived experience of the world is incorporated and realized and, as such, is neither pure object nor pure subject. The body is neither pure object, since it is the place of one's engagement with the world; nor is it pure subject, in that there is always a material residue that resists incorporation into dominant symbolic schema. In Elizabeth Grosz's words (1994a), the body is a 'transitional entity'. A lack of corporeal finality arises from a mutual inherence between psychical interior and corporeal exterior where each is constitutive but not reducible to the other. Such a lack of finality suggests, for example, that the ascription of feminine corporeal identity is never straightforward or complete. The idea of a dynamic and non-dichotomous inherence between the body and subjectivity is important for feminist theory because it allows a recognition of the central, but not invariant, role played by sexuality in women's incorporated experience of the world. A fluid relation to gendered identity is implied where gender norms are understood as entrenched but not unsurpassable boundaries. Embodiment expresses a moment of indeterminacy whereby the embodied subject is constituted through dominant norms but is not reducible to them.

In this area, it is the work of Judith Butler that has perhaps had the most influence. Butler's formulation of the idea of the performative attempts to move beyond understanding the construction of gender identity as a one-sided process of imposition or determination by thinking of it in terms of the temporally more open process of repetition. Repetition denotes both a process of profound corporeal inscription and also a fundamental instability at the heart of dominant gender norms. Rather than thinking of gender as a quasi-permanent structure, she claims that it should be thought of as the *temporalized regulation* of socio-symbolic norms and practices where the idea of the performative expresses both the cultural arbitrariness or 'performed' nature of gender identity and also its deep inculcation in that every performance serves to reinscribe it upon the body. Performativity does not refer to a voluntarist process of performance so much as a 'forced reiteration of norms' in the sense of a compulsory and constraining heterosexuality that impels and sustains gender identity (Butler 1993a: 94). Although constraint is the condition of possibility of sexuality, this does not mean that the cultural imperative of hetero-sexual norms is inexorable. Change arises from the constitut-ive instability of the symbolic and discursive structures which invest the body with meaning. The cultural necessity for a performative reiteration of these symbolic norms highlights the extent to which they are not natural or inevitable and are, therefore, potentially open to change through processes of resignification.

By emphasizing the historicity of structure, the concept of the performative highlights how constraint is constitutive but not fully determining of gender subjectivity; in other words, a space for agency is outlined. Butler's account of agency relies on Foucault's idea of 'subjectivation' which denotes the dialec-tical aspect of identity formation, that 'the subject is consti-tuted through practices of subjection, or, in a more autonomous way, through practices of liberation, of liberty' (Foucault 1988: 50). Despite this insight, Butler, along with others, notes that Foucault himself does not elaborate sufficiently on the specific mechanisms whereby the subject is formed in submission but is never reducible to it, as the idea of subjects as 'docile bodies' seems to imply (Butler 1997b: 2). In order to overcome this difficulty, Butler bases the idea of performative agency on an understanding of temporality not as a series of discrete, punctuated moments, but rather as a process of *materialization* in which the constraints of social structures are reproduced and partially transcended in the practices of agents: 'construction . . . is itself a temporal process which operates through the reiteration of norms; sex is both produced and destabilized in the course of this reiteration' (Butler 1993a: 10). Agency is a sedimented effect of reiterative or ritualized practices; the re-peated inscription of the symbolic norms of heterosexuality upon the body and the living through of those norms permits the emergence of a stable bodily ego (1993a: 14). The perform-ative construction of gender identity causes agency in that the identificatory processes, through which norms are materi-alized, permits the stabilization of a subject who is capable of resisting those norms. This process of resistance takes place primarily at the boundaries of the corporeal norm, in the domains of 'excluded and delegitimated' sex (1993a: 16). The partial and conflictual identifications made by those who are excluded from a heterosexual regime can result in a destabilizing process of *resignification* in which symbolic norms are subversively used to articulate homosexual identities evident, for example, in queer practices.

Butler's idea of performative agency has had an enormous impact upon feminist work on gender identity (e.g. Bell et al. 1994; Bell 1999; Pellegrini 1997). It has also provoked considerable debate and criticism, much of which circulates around the question of the extent to which the idea of the performative elaborated by Butler and others does in fact offer a reworked conception of agency. In the final analysis, these criticisms can be related to difficulties with the underdeveloped idea of agency that arises in the negative paradigm of subjectification within whose terms the idea of the performative is elaborated. Despite her awareness of the shortcomings in Foucault's work, in many ways Butler replicates its failure to integrate a theory of agency with an understanding of the disciplinary inscription of the body. Foucault's much noted conflation of individuals with docile bodies forecloses an explanation of notions such as agency and praxis which are central to an understanding of the indeterminacies of gender relations.[1] In a similar fashion, the priority accorded to the moment of constraint by Butler is evident in her account of the temporality of the performative which is thematized mainly as a property of sedimented symbolic structures rather than as an anticipatory element inherent in praxis. It is also evident in her failure to connect the symbolic construction of the body to other material relations in which this process takes place. Despite claims that it is traversed by a multiplicity of heterogeneous power relations, a rather undifferentiated and formal account of the symbolic order emerges as the realm of uniform normativity. This, in turn, sets in play a series of dualisms which limit an understanding of agency. In order to consider these issues in more detail, however, the implications of

Bourdieu's work on habitus for a theory of gender identity will now be discussed.

Habitus and symbolic domination

In the light of certain difficulties with Foucault's work on subjectification and agency and the move in feminism towards a more dynamic conceptualization of embodied existence, it is perhaps surprising that the work of Pierre Bourdieu on habitus and *le sens pratique* has not received more attention. In a manner similar to Foucault, habitus expresses the idea that bodily identity is not natural but involves the inscription of dominant social norms or the 'cultural arbitrary' upon the body. For both thinkers, the body lies at the centre of modern strategies of social control. However, for Bourdieu, the concept of habitus does not denote just the process in which norms are inculcated upon the body, but also the moment of praxis or living through of these norms by the individual. This temporalization of a concept of bodily existence means that, unlike the idea of disciplinary power, habitus is defined not as a determining principle, but as a *generative* structure. The centrality of temporality to the idea of habitus elucidates more fully how agency emerges from the somatization of power relations, overcoming some of the difficulties of the Foucauldian reduction of individuals to docile bodies.

Bourdieu, like Foucault, claims that large-scale social inequalities are established, not at the level of direct institutional discrimination, but through the subtle inculcation of power relations upon the bodies and dispositions of individuals. This process of corporeal inculcation is an instance of what Bourdieu calls *symbolic violence* or a form of domination which is 'exercised upon a social agent with his or her complicity' (1992: 167). The incorporation of the social into the corporeal is captured by Bourdieu in the idea of habitus, a system of durable, transposable dispositions that mediates the actions of an individual and the external conditions of production (1990a: 53). An institution can only be efficacious if it is objectified in bodies in the form of durable dispositions that recognize and comply with the specific demands of a given institutional area of activity, 'the habitus is what enables the institution to attain full realization' (1990a: 57).

In the article 'La domination masculine' (1990b), Bourdieu looks at what he considers to be the paradigm of symbolic domination, namely gender inequality (1992: 170). Drawing on his research into the North African society of Kabyle, Bourdieu shows how masculine domination assumes a natural, self-evident status through its inscription in the objective structures of the social world which are then incorporated and reproduced in the habitus of individuals. The key to the naturalization of the masculine–feminine opposition is its insertion in a series of analogous oppositions – a 'mythico-ritual' system – which occludes the arbitrary nature of the sexual division by lending it a 'semantic' thickness or an overdetermination of connotations and correspondences. These binaries are lived and reinvoked in the everyday life of the Kabyle and are particularly evident in the structuring of the social space which confines women, by and large, to circumscribed domestic, pastoral and market locations as opposed to the masculine sites of the public sphere.

The inscription of a system of sexualized oppositions upon social space is paralleled in the 'somatization' of these relations within the bodies of individuals. Hierarchical gender relations are embedded in bodily *hexis*, that is to say, arbitrary power relations are inculcated upon the body in the naturalized form of gender identity. The living through of bodily hexis leads to doxic forms of perception which permit the 're-engenderization' of all perceived social differences, that is, their interpretation in a sexualized dualism. Thus women become implicated within a circular logic where the cultural arbitrary is imposed upon the body in a naturalized form whose cognitive effects (*doxa*) result in the further naturalization of arbitrary social differences. Women in Kabyle society realize in their conduct the negative identity that has been socially imposed upon them and in doing so naturalize this identity (1990b: 10). Although Kabyle is a peasant culture, Bourdieu claims it provides a limit case paradigm of the basic processes of somatization through which sexual divisions are maintained in modern industrial society.

Le sens pratique and gender

At first sight, the idea of embodiment expressed in the notion
of habitus appears not to be a dynamic, open-ended process,
but rather one of inexorable physical control not dissimilar to
the Foucauldian notion of discipline. On this view, it is unclear how a notion of agency may be developed. Indeed, the
charge of determinism is a common criticism of Bourdieu's
work (e.g. Alexander 1994: 136; Garnham and Williams 1980:
222). These criticisms fail to recognize fully, however, the
force of Bourdieu's insistence that habitus is not to be conceived
as a principle of determination but as a generative structure.
Within certain objective limits (the *field*), habitus engenders a
potentially infinite number of patterns of behaviour, thought
and expression that are both 'relatively unpredictable' but also
'limited in their diversity'. Thus, habitus gives practice a relative autonomy with respect to the external determinations of
the immediate present but, at the same time, ensures that it is
objectively adapted to its outcomes (1990a: 55). The temporalization of habitus, expressed in its inseparability from a notion
of praxis, is key to understanding how Bourdieu conceptualizes it as a generative structure.

The generative nature of the habitus is grounded in what
Bourdieu calls a 'double and obscure' relation between individual habitus and the social circumstances or 'field' from which
it emerges. On one side, there is a relation of conditioning
where the objective conditions of a given field structure the
habitus. On the other, there is a relation of 'cognitive construction' whereby habitus is constitutive of the field in that it
endows the latter with meaning, with 'sense and value', in
which it is worth investing one's energy' (1992: 127). This
dialogical relation can be understood in temporal terms where
the incorporation into the body of objective tendencies of the
world is lived as seemingly natural physical and emotional dispositions. However, the uncertainties and anticipatory elements
immanent in the way in which these potentialities are lived
renders this an active, interpretative process rather than a merely
repetitive one. This future-oriented or anticipatory dimension

is defined, in Husserlian terms, as protension; the positing of a future immediately inscribed in the present, 'an objective potentiality . . . endowed with the doxic modality of the present' (Bourdieu 1990c: 109). In so far as meaningful social action is what Crespi (1989) calls a 'borderline concept' – that is, it is neither fully determined nor fully willed – the habitus is a generative rather than determining structure which establishes an active and creative relation – *'ars inveniendi'* (1992: 122) – between the subject and the world.

Habitus is realized in *le sens pratique* (feel for the game) a pre-reflexive level of practical mastery (1990a: 52). It is a mode of knowledge that does not necessarily contain know-ledge of its own principles (*docta ignoratia*) and is constitutive of reasonable but not rational behaviour (1990c: 109). 'It is because agents never know completely what they are doing that what they do has more sense than they know' (1990a: 69). The example, taken from Merleau Ponty, that Bourdieu frequently uses to explain the concept is of the tennis player whose strokes are spontaneous and relatively unpredictable in a match despite being consciously and mechanically practised beforehand. *Le sens pratique* is a form of knowledge that is learnt by the body but cannot be explicitly articulated.

To explain gender identity in terms of this notion of 'pract-ical belief' is to suggest that it amounts to something more than the internalization of an external set of representations by a subject. The acquisition of gender identity does not pass through consciousness; it is not memorized but enacted at a pre-reflexive level. At the same time, bodily dispositions are not simply inscribed or mechanically learnt but lived as a form of 'practical mimesis': 'the body believes in what it plays at: it weeps if it mimes grief' (1990a: 73). In his critique of the con-cept of ideology, Foucault also draws attention to the way in which disciplinary power does not pass through consciousness (Foucault 1980: 186). However, the absence, in his oeuvre, of a more developed notion of the acting subject means that the idea of discipline does not go far beyond a technical principle of bodily constraint. A similar notion of a protensive temporal-ity is missing in some constructionist accounts of gender iden-tity which, as a consequence, tend to offer rather overstated

explanations of corporeal determination. This is evident, for
example, in Foucault's account, in the first volume of *The
History of Sexuality*, of the 'hysterization' of the female body
which is construed in such uni-directional terms that it is difficult to see how, despite considerable constraints, women were
able to resist such processes and to act independently (Foucault
1978: 104).

Habitus and the performative

By elaborating some of the temporal implications of the dialectic of subjectification, significant similarities are established
between Bourdieu's idea of habitus and Butler's work on the
materialization of gender norms. Both thinkers deploy a
notion of 'double historicity' in order to escape from uni-
directional determinist accounts of identity formation and
to formulate an alternative account of agency (Bourdieu 1992:
139). In Butler, the possibility of agency emerges in the moment of indeterminacy inherent to the process of reiteration.
In Bourdieu, this double historicity is expressed in terms of the
Husserlian themes of retention and protension which yield a
dynamic account of embodied existence and agency. In contrast with the atemporality of the Foucauldian *tabula rasa*, an
understanding of embodiment as inseparable from social practice leads Bourdieu to speak of social agents rather than subjects (1992: 137). Praxis, or the living through of the embodied
potentialities of the habitus, is a temporal activity where time
is understood in radically historicist terms as engendered
through social being. Practice is the result of a habitus that is
itself the incorporation of temporal structures or the regularities and tendencies of the world into the body. Embodied
practice is necessarily temporal in that it both expresses and
anticipates these tendencies and regularities. Practice, therefore, generates time: 'time is engendered in the actualisation of
the act' (1992: 138). By conceiving of habitus as a temporal
structure, the body is imputed a dynamism and mutability.

At the same time, the stress on the anticipatory dimension
to the process of subjectification is counterbalanced by an

insistence on the pre-reflexive and sedimented aspects of incorporated existence. This is necessary to bypass the voluntarism or intentionalism that hampers certain understandings of identity. Although ultimately there are difficulties in maintaining a clear division between the idea of the performative and the more intentionalist notion of performance, Butler emphasizes that the former is not, in any sense, to be understood as a willed construction of identity (1993a: x). The idea of habitus also suggests a layer of embodied experience that is not immediately amenable to self-fashioning. On a pre-reflexive level, the actor is predisposed or oriented to behave in a certain way because of the 'active-presence' of the whole past embedded in the durable structures of the habitus. The pre-reflexive mode of habitus provides a more differentiated or layered account of the entrenched dimensions of embodied experiences that might escape processes of reflexive self-monitoring. Thus, detraditionalizing forces may have thrown certain aspects of gender relations – the gender division of labour, marriage – up for renegotiation. At the same time, however, men and women have deep-seated, often unconscious investments in conventional images of masculinity and femininity which cannot easily be reshaped and throw into doubt certain recent ideas of the transformation of intimacy. The destabilizing of conventional gender relations on one level may further entrench, in a reactive fashion, conventional patterns of behaviour on other levels. For example, women's entry into the workforce has not freed women demonstrably from the burden of emotional responsibilities. Rather it has made the process of female individualization more complex in that the notion of 'living one's own life' is in a conflictual relation with the conventional expectation of 'being there for others' (Beck and Beck-Gernsheim 1995: 22). In a similar vein, work on the sociology of emotions suggests that despite modernizing forces, gender differences in emotional behaviour are deeply entrenched (Duncombe and Marsden 1993).

Such discontinuities between pre-reflexive and reflexive modes of behaviour are often overlooked in recent work in identity transformation. Work by Anthony Giddens on reflexivity and the transformation of intimacy, for example, is characterized by a relative lack of concern for the issue of embodiment (Turner 1991: 11). Whilst he is careful to temper his discussion of the transformatory potential of reflexive self-management with an emphasis on a reactive ontological anxiety, Giddens concentrates on the existential rather than corporeal aspects of identity. His discussion of sexuality in *The Transformation of Intimacy* is construed in the largely abstract terms of the 'sequestration of experience' and its implications of affectual and moral anomie. While Giddens is rightly critical of Foucault's overlooking of the affectual and cognitive aspects of sexuality by reducing identity to an effect of biopower, he, in turn, tends to disregard the involuntary, prereflexive and entrenched elements in subjectivity. Without having to resort to biologistic notions of maternal instinct, the inscription of the mothering role upon the female body is fundamental in the inculcation of emotional and physical predispositions that maintain gender inequality around childrearing. It is not clear how such forms of identity, which are overdetermined both physically and emotionally, can be easily dislodged (Soper 1990: 60). It is in the light of such concerns that Giddens's claim that 'revolutionary processes are already under way in the infrastructure of personal life' seem to require much qualification (Giddens 1992: 182). In sum, there is a tendency in certain theories of identity transformation to conceive of identity solely as a mode of symbolic identification without considering its mediation in embodied practices (e.g. Featherstone 1992).

A weakness of certain theories of reflexive transformation is that the emphasis placed upon strategic and conscious processes of self-monitoring overlooks certain more enduring, reactive aspects of identity or, as Bourdieu puts it, the extent to which the habitus continues to work long after the objective conditions of its emergence have been dislodged (1990b: 13). For example, certain theories of reflexive transformation place much weight on 'biographically significant life choices' whilst ignoring the 'unconsidered and automatic, habitual routine of conduct' (Campbell 1996: 163). As Bourdieu points out, 'determinisms operate to their full only by the help of unconsciousness' (1992: 136). Whilst gender identity is not an immutable or essential horizon, there are many pre-reflexive aspects of masculine and feminine behaviour – sexual desire, maternal feelings – that call into question the process of identity transformation highlighted by some theories of reflexivity. This is a result of the deeply entrenched nature of gender identity and also of the way in which gender as a primary symbolic distinction is used to play out other social tensions. As Bourdieu shows in *Distinction*, anxieties about class status and belonging are sublimated into and played out through the categories of masculinity and femininity, thereby entrenching them further (1979: 382).

While Butler and Bourdieu attempt to break from an intentionalist account of agency, both also share a resistance to understanding the pre-reflexive formation of subjectivity in psychoanalytical terms. Both thinkers adduce the constructionist objection that psychoanalysis reifies the structures of gender identity and forecloses an account of agency. By gesturing towards potentially unrecuperable elements of embodied experience, Bourdieu and Butler share with psychoanalysis a stress on the priority of originary experiences which lead to a *relative* closure or sedimentation of the systems of disposition constitutive of habitus (1992: 134). A difficulty for a feminist appropriation of psychoanalytic theory is that this closure appears to be immutable in so far as the symbolic realm is understood in psychic rather than socio-historical terms, resulting in the the problem of construing feminine positions as anything other than invariable negativity (see chapter 4). Thus, for Butler, Lacan's reification of the symbolic realm as an immutable law forecloses 'the complex crossings of identification' which might contest its phallocentric terms (1993: 103). In order to permit the possibility of resistance, the symbolic order has to be understood in more sociocentric terms as the realm where heterogeneous power relations are partially stabilized but through citational practices and not through being grounded in the presocial structure of the psyche (1993: 106). Similarly, in Bourdieu, although the habitus accords a disproportionate weight to primary social experiences, the resulting closure is never absolute because the habitus is a historical structure that is only ever realized in reference to specific situations. Thus, while an agent might be predisposed to act in certain ways, the potentiality for innovation or creative action is never foreclosed: '[habitus] is an *open system of dispositions* that is constantly subjected to experiences, and therefore constantly affected by them in a way that either reinforces or modifies its structures' (1992: 133). While psychoanalysis provides a more nuanced account of the ambivalences that surround the ac-quistion of gender identity, Bourdieu is critical of the way in which its archetypal psycho-sexual categories cannot account for the myriad of other social power relations – 'the countless acts of diffuse inculcation through which the body and the world tend to be set in order' – that are superincumbent and may run counter to sexual division (1990a: 78). By drawing out certain temporal aspects to the process of embodiment, the ideas of habitus and the performative open up a theoret-ical space for agency and for an explanation of the elements of variability and potential creativity immanent to even the most routine reproduction of gender identity.

Praxis and indeterminacy

Despite the affinities between their work on temporality and the body, Butler has worked mainly within a Foucauldian para-digm and has only recently engaged with Bourdieu's work (1997a). On the whole, her interpretation of Bourdieu's work has been negative in that she criticizes the idea of symbolic violence as being so skewed towards explaining the reproduc-tion of the status quo that it misses the instability of dominant forms which render them open to subversion and resignification. Against this, it can be argued that the theory of agency that Butler presents is, in fact, a structural abstraction rather than an account of the logic of practice. The instability of symbolic systems, which is a central premise of the idea of the per-formative, forms the condition of possibility of agency but says little about the complex of power relations, symbolic and material, that give rise to political action. Ultimately, Butler's failure to offer a more substantive account of agency can be related to her remaining within an essentially negative paradigm

of subjectification which privileges an idea of structural indeterminacy over that of praxis. This contrasts with the more
generative idea of habitus whose more explicit formulation
of a dialectical temporality yields a praxeological account of
agency.

The persistence of the negative paradigm of subjectification
in Butler's work is evident in the tendency to explore temporality mainly through the retroactive dimension of sedimentation. Although Butler briefly acknowledges the presence of a
potentially disruptive temporality at the heart of the most
regulatory norms, the notion of performativity seems closer to
a version of the Freudian idea of repetition compulsion, which
is essentially a reactive and, according to some commentators,
an atemporal concept (see R. Smith 1996). The emphasis on
the retrospective dimensions of time – the performative as 'a
repetition, a sedimentation, a congealment of the past' (Butler
1993a: 244) – leads to a rather exaggerated notion of the
internal uniformity of gender norms. Thus, the destabilizing
force of the idea of reiteration is undercut and becomes a
static rather than temporal act where the reproduction of the
sex–gender system involves a ceaseless reinscription of the
same. This notion of time as a succession of self-identical and
discrete acts renders the dominant order hermetic and self-
sustaining and means that disruption only appears to come from
outside the norm, from the domain of the abject, understood
as '"unlivable" and "uninhabitable" zones of social life' (Butler
1993a: 3). In short, the one-dimensional notion of temporality as
sedimentation results in a monolithic account of the 'normal'
and tacitly reinvokes dualisms of domination and resistance,
the normal and the excluded, and so forth.

This latent dualism of the normal and the excluded in Butler's
work is reinforced by the structural rather than 'praxeological'
account of temporality that is deployed.[2] Agency is conceived
of as the inherent indeterminacy of symbolic structures rather
than as the result of social practice. In the performative, there
is no subject who precedes the reiteration of norms, rather it is
the latter which *'precede, constrain, and exceed the performer and
in that sense cannot be taken as a fabrication of the performer's
"will" or "choice"'* (1993b: 24) In other words, a formal account

of the conditions of possibility of agency is substituted for a more explicitly praxeological understanding of agency. In Butler, agency remains an abstract structural potentiality which is sufficiently undifferentiated that it becomes difficult, for example, to distinguish whether an act is politically effective or not given that all identity is performatively constructed (e.g. Lloyd 1999). Butler's explanation of the indeterminacy of the symbolic process of materialization provides an account of the necessary structural conditions that give rise to agency. It lacks, however, a sufficient understanding of how the performative aspects of gender identity are lived by individuals in relation to the web of social practices in which they are enmeshed. Moreover, the claim that the performative may acquire 'act-like status' does not go much further in explaining how the idea of agency is little more than a structural abstraction which, as Fraser puts it, is 'deeply antihumanist' (Fraser 1995: 67).[3] In so far as it appears to be primarily a capacity of symbolic structures rather than of individuals, Butler's idea of agency lacks social and historical specificity.[4] An implication of this abstract account of subject formation is that an analysis of the political dimensions of agency – the capacity of individuals to engender change within the socio-cultural order – is not fully explored. For example, the latent dualism, operating in her work, of signification versus resignification is far from adequate in capturing the complex dynamics of social change. Indeed, the effect is an absolutization of change where the act of resignification becomes valorized in itself.

By considering the interplay of retention–protention from a praxeological perspective, Bourdieu is able to explain more clearly than Butler how it is that the agent emerges from an originary act of subordination. The somatization of power relations involves the imposition of limits upon the body which simultaneously constitute the condition of possibility of agency. Agency is an act of temporalization where the subject transcends the present through actions that have an inherently anticipatory structure. The practical activity of the agent transcends the immediacy of the present through the 'mobilization of the past and practical anticipation of the future inscribed in the present in a state of objective potentiality' (Bourdieu 1992:

138). The intertwinement of corporeal being and agency implied in the concept of habitus transcends the opposition between freedom and constraint characteristic, for example, of liberal conceptions of the subject. Foucault (1982: 221) also argues against an understanding of the subject in terms of an antinomy of freedom and constraint; however, the lack of a praxeological concept of temporality to mediate the moments of determinism and voluntarism in his thought prevents him from developing this insight. For Bourdieu, the formation of subjectivity within a symbolic system involves subjection to dominant power relations, but also involves the institution of meaning. The instantiation of a subject within dominatory power relations does not negate but rather implies agency: 'I do not see how relations of domination . . . could possibly operate without implying, activating resistance. *The dominated, in any social universe, can always exert a certain force,* inasmuch as belonging to a field means by definition that one is capable of producing effects in it' (1992: 80). In this way, the relation between symbolic structure and subject is shifted from an antinomy of domination–resistance to a more differentiated concept of 'regulated liberties' (1991: 102).

Speech and conduct

The abstract account of agency and the absolutization of change that are consequences of Butler's idea of the performative signal a further problematic tendency to privilege a symbolic account of subjectification over an examination of its material dimensions. The subsumption of the material within the symbolic has a correlate in the reduction of the broader issue of gender hierarchies to that of the construction of sexual identity. The effect of this is that agency is narrowly conceived in terms of linguistic effects or as positionality within language and is operationalised often only in the delimited realm of sexuality (e.g. Benhabib 1995; Fraser 1995).

In *Excitable Speech*, Butler addresses this issue of her alleged conflation of the material with the symbolic through a re-elaboration of the notion of performative agency in terms of speech-act theory. The criticism of the lack of socio-historical specificity in the idea of the performative is dealt with through an insistence on the importance of the distinction between the symbolic and practice – 'speech and conduct' – in order not to conflate the existence of hegemonic norms with the ways in which they may be taken up and modified in the practices of social actors. By distinguishing the material from the symbolic in this way, Butler offers a revivified account of political agency.

Excitable Speech is based around the central thesis that speech is always, to some degree, out of control, rendering it suscept-ible to processes of unauthorized appropriation and, hence, resignification. Recognition of this instability – the *excitability* of discourse – frees speech from the all-encompassing inten-tionality of the putative sovereign subject. A space is thereby opened for an alternative conception of agency in terms of a counter-discourse that acknowledges its emergence from and dependency upon structures of constraint: 'agency begins where sovereignty wanes. The one who acts . . . acts precisely to the extent that he or she is constituted as an actor and, hence, operating within a linguistic field of enabling constraints from the outset' (1997a: 16).

This concept of agency underscores the indeterminacy inherent in even the most violent and oppressive forms of dis-course or hate speech and is sustained through the distinction between illocutionary and perlocutionary performatives. The former are speech acts that enact what they are saying in the moment of saying whereas, in the latter, certain effects follow from, rather than being synchronous with, the act of speech. Following Derrida's critique of Austin, Butler demonstrates the incoherence of understanding the illocutionary act as that which executes its deed at the moment of utterance by argu-ing that its performative power relies on forms of ceremonial, ritual and convention whose necessarily prior status undoes the idea of the single, self-contained moment of performance. The instantaneity of effect is undone by the existence of structures that predate and outlast the performative: 'The "moment" in ritual is a condensed historicity: it exceeds itself in past and future directions, an effect of prior and future in-vocations that constitute and escape the instance of utterance'

(1997a: 3). In Butler's view, Austin's understanding of illocutionary force rests on an untenable conflation of utterance with
effect, or speech with conduct. Although it has corporeal effects,
the injury of speech cannot be as immediate as that of physical
assault; rather it operates through a process of temporal deferral where its repeated effects bring into being or materialize
derogated subject positions. Interpellation of the subject is not
an instantaneous act of subjection, but involves a process of
cultural reiteration which engenders a somatic circuit of recognition. The process of temporal deferral, where the original
conditions of utterance cannot be indefinitely sustained, points
also to the possibility of the intentionality of the utterance
going awry and producing unintended effects of subversion
and counter-discourse. The open temporality of speech results
in a dissemination of effects beyond the control of the speaking subject that may result in the possibility of resignification,
or the 'subject's linguistic survival as well as, potentially, that
subject's linguistic death' (1997a: 28).

Although it suggests a dialogical account of the subject's
location with regard to dominant norms, it may appear that,
rather than moving towards a more distinct understanding of
political agency, the idea of the perlocutionary effects of the
performative entrenches itself deeper within a primarily linguistic account of subject formation. Butler goes on, however,
to draw out some of the problematic political implications
that a closing of the gap between speech and its effects has
upon the political analysis of 'hate speech'. Catherine
MacKinnon, for example, understands the effects of pornography in terms of the illocutionary performative, that is, that
hate speech constitutes its addressee at the moment of utterance. Pornography does not reinforce patriarchal structures;
it constructs women's social reality in the form of a visual
imperative which compels a compliance with its demand: 'the
image says, "do this", where the commanded act is an act of
sexual subordination, and where, in the doing of that act, the
social reality of woman is constructed precisely as the position
of the sexually subordinate' (Butler 1997a: 67). The problem
with such an analysis is that it places the objects of porno-
graphic representation so unambiguously in the position of

victim that it denies the agency of the oppressed. This is evident in MacKinnon's categorical refusal to recognize that lesbian and gay pornography does not simply replicate structures of victimization, but, in fact, has emancipatory implications for those whose sexuality is denied public expression. Furthermore, this collapsing of speech with its effects justifies strategies of state intervention, such as censorship, on behalf of those who are presumed to be unable to act for themselves. As Foucault has recognized, the intensification of juridical control in areas such as sexuality is used often against the very social movements and marginal groups it is meant to protect.

The insistence on the gap between speech and conduct, then, does not represent a retreat by Butler into abstruse linguistic theory, but rather broadens an understanding of political agency beyond institutional and juridical arenas, giving support to 'ways of restaging and resignifying speech in contexts that exceed those determined by the courts' (1997a: 23). It is precisely this more diffuse idea of agency arising from the potential for resignification which, in Butler's view, Bourdieu's concept of symbolic violence fails to capture. From her perspective, the problem with the concept of symbolic violence is that it ties the speech act too closely to its institutional context and misses the processes of temporal deferral and dissemination that are constitutive of the indeterminacy of the performative and of the potential for misappropriation. Such a criticism echoes those of commentators who claim that Bourdieu's theory is so skewed towards explaining social reproduction that it is unable to offer an account of change or disruption within the social structure (e.g. Alexander 1994). A lack of indeterminacy is said to hamper Bourdieu's notion of habitus which, by stressing the extent to which there is an accommodation between dominant power relations and bodily dispositions, misses the extent to which the process of corporeal inculcation is never straightforward or complete. There is a residue, or bodily volatility, that renders strategies of domination vulnerable to displacement: 'This excess is what Bourdieu's account appears to miss or, perhaps, to suppress: the abiding incongruity of the speaking body, the way in which it exceeds its interpellation, and remains uncontained by any of its acts of speech' (Butler 1997a: 155). By producing an account of power that is structurally committed to the status quo, Bourdieu forecloses the possibility of agency emerging from the margins. In contrast, the idea of the performative draws attention to how institutionalized forms of recognition and a critical perspective on existing institutions are simultaneously produced, for example, in calls for justice or democracy on the part of those who have been radically disenfranchised.

Butler rightly draws attention to a tendency in Bourdieu's work to overestimate the accommodation between dominant symbolic codes and corporeal hexis. Yet, against Butler, this tendency need not be regarded as inherent to the concepts of habitus and symbolic violence *per se*, but rather arises from a failure on Bourdieu's part to integrate sufficiently these concepts with his idea of the field. It is the refractory and destabilizing implications that the concept of the field has for the notion of habitus which are overlooked and which allow Bourdieu to produce a more nuanced understanding of power relations and political agency than Butler's primarily symbolic account of subjectification. In order to understand agency in terms other than the dualisms of domination and resistance or signification and resignification, it is essential to theorize the various material relations through which symbolic norms are mediated. If difference is understood not just as symbolic indeterminacy but as the interplay between differentiated relations of power, then a theoretical space is created for a more substantive account of agency predicated on a negotiation of social complexity. To enable a more detailed discussion of the implications of the concept of the field for an understanding of gender and agency, however, it is necessary first to consider the occasions where Bourdieu neglects to draw out fully the force of the concept of the field for the idea of habitus. This is most evident in his extended essay on masculine domination, which, by failing to consider gender identity in the context of differentiated power relations, results in a dualist account of sexual division.

Masculine domination

In pointing towards the rootedness of gender divisions in social forms, Bourdieu's concepts of habitus and *le sens pratique* do not necessarily exclude the possibility of agency or attendant possibilities for politically motivated change. The potential for change is immanent to the temporally open nature of social praxis as it is mediated through the increasingly differentiated nature of modern society into distinct fields of action. The field is defined as a network or configuration of objective relations between positions (1993: 72–7). The configuration receives its form from the relation between each position and the distribution of a certain type of capital. Capital – economic, social, cultural and symbolic – denotes the different goods, resources and values around which power relations in a particular field crystallize. Any field is marked by a tension or conflict between the interests of different groups who struggle to gain control over a field's capital. In the final instance, all fields are determined by the demands of the capitalist system of accumulation; however, each field is autonomous in that it has a specific internal logic which establishes non-synchronous, uneven relations with other fields and which renders it irreducible to any overarching dynamic.

The proliferation of differentiated fields of action leads to a 'lengthening of circuits of legitimation' which has both positive and negative effects. In an argument that resembles Foucault's critique of monarchical concepts of power, Bourdieu claims that when power is no longer incarnated in persons or specific institutions but becomes coextensive with a complex set of relations between different fields, social control becomes more insidious and hence more effective. At the same time, this increase in the efficacy of symbolic domination is counterbalanced by an increase in 'the potential for subversive misappropriation' arising from movement and conflict between fields of action (1989: 554–7).

Although Bourdieu considers the destabilizing and potentially subversive effects that might arise from movement across fields – for example, with regard to the migration of peasants from rural to urban areas – he fails to extend this insight to his work on the construction of modern gender identity. To put this in other terms, the conceptual implications of the idea of the field are not brought to bear sufficiently on the idea of the gendered habitus. While habitus draws attention to the entrenched nature of gender identity, it is important to consider the extent to which its effects may be attenuated by the movement of individuals across fields. If the differentiation of society leads to what Luhmann (1986) calls an 'a priori displacement' of individuals, the lack of fit between gendered habitus and field may be intensified. Such a consideration is imperative in the light of the increased entry of women into traditionally non-feminine spheres of action and in the light of the putative opening up of alternative definitions of masculinity that some theorists have identified (e.g. Segal 1990). In his studies of specific fields of action, Bourdieu alludes to possible dimensions of such changes. For example, in *La noblesse d'Etat*, he mentions the correlation between women's increased entry into higher education and declining levels of fertility, but the broader implications for an understanding of the construction of gender identity are not considered. More strikingly, in his only sustained consideration of gender identity, the extended essay entitled 'La domination masculine', the concept of the field is not discussed (1989: 390–2).

The origin of this oversight in Bourdieu's work lies in his extrapolation of the 'basic mythic structures' of sexuality from an analysis of Kabyle society. Despite the recognition, in principle, that a pure dualism of sexual difference must be attenuated, to some degree, in a differentiated society, Bourdieu claims that these archaic mental structures still survive in contemporary practices and dispositions (1990b: 4). Contemporary masculinity is construed as the enactment of the *libido dominandi*, an unfaltering assertion of virility which pits men against each other in agonistic games of self-assertion. Masculine privilege is a trap in as much as: 'the dominant is dominated by his domination' (1992: 173). The principle of *isotimie* – equality in honour – that governs these games of masculine competition excludes the feminine entirely. This exclusion from the realm of masculine privilege accords women a certain critical insight – the 'lucidity of the excluded' – into masculinity. However, their subordinate position means that women remain complicit with these games, and thus participate by proxy (*par procuration*) in their own subordination and serve as 'flattering mirrors' to the games of men (1990b: 26).

Although he rightly stresses the ingrained nature of gender norms, Bourdieu significantly underestimates the ambiguities and dissonances that exist in the way that men and women occupy masculine and feminine positions. The lack of a sustained consideration of gendered habitus in relation to the field results in an overemphasis on the alignment that the habitus establishes between subjective dispositions and the objective structure of the field with regard to gender identity. In a recently reworked version of the essay on masculine domination, Bourdieu acknowledges the changes in women's social status resulting from their movement out of the domestic sphere (Bourdieu 1999: 95–101). He is, at the same time, cautious about the extent to which women's entry into previously male-dominated fields of action represents an absolute increase in autonomy, pointing to the persistance of male–female inequalities across all social fields. Yet, any attempt to map out the complex nature of relations of autonomy and dependence within and across fields is persistently undercut by what he sees as the prior, determining force of the transhistorical, invariant principle of masculine domination (1999: 11–115). This tension between the assertion of a universal, gendered habitus and the historical specificity of relations within a given field remains unresolved and results in a monolithic account of the reproduction of gender relations. An invariable alignment is posited between the masculine and feminine dispositions and the demands of social reproduction. This alignment is regarded as so stable that it leads Bourdieu to claim that the phallonarcissistic view of the world can only be dislodged through complete rejection of the gendered habitus (1990b: 30). There is no recognition that apparent complicity can conceal potential dislocation or alienation on the part of individuals. It is precisely such dislocation and instabilities within the construction of the gendered subject to which Butler and other feminists draw attention. For example, Janet Radway's

(1987) study of women readers of romance fiction, *Reading the Romance*, shows that what might appear initially as a passive act of identification with highly conventional images of masculinity and femininity is in fact motivated by a more active attempt by women to work through the disappointments and tensions arising from their attempts to negotiate the competing feminine roles of mother, wife and worker. Radway's study presents a far more complex picture of contemporary gender relations than Bourdieu's notion of masculine domination and female complicity. It also highlights the importance of a hermeneutic perspective – lacking in this part of Bourdieu's work – in grasping the attitudes and investments that underlie broader cultural shifts.

In a similar fashion, recent work on masculinities has revealed that with regard to 'dominant' forms of subjectivity, the habitus cannot be said always to ensure unproblematic alignment between the demands of the field and subjective dispositions. Kaja Silverman (1992), for example, has argued that the dominant conception of masculinity is an idealized fiction and is, therefore, a position that cannot be filled within the social realm. Just as, according to Lacan, the notion of the feminine is unfillable because of its negative relation to the symbolic, so the masculine, as the epicentre of meaning in a phallocentric system, is an abiding illusion. As the moment of absolute presence in the symbolic, masculine identity rests on an impossible adequation of the biological penis with the phallus. Using a similar idea of masculinity as an imaginary and hence unfillable place, Marjorie Garber (1992) argues that attempts to occupy the position of the masculine must result in a degree of feminization because of their inevitable failure. Developing Lacan's assertion that virile display in the human being has a feminine aspect, Garber claims that the real male cannot be embodied at all, that embodiment itself is a form of feminization. In a study of male icons (Valentino, Elvis, etc.), Garber shows how fetishized images of masculinity bear within them the traces of the feminized man-transvestite and thus point towards their own constitutive instability and possible displacement.

The instability of the categories of masculinity and femininity need not necessarily be construed as a crisis within contemporary identity formations. Nor can they unambiguously be invested with political significance, *pace* Butler, given the capacity of capitalist systems for containment through commodification. As Žižek puts it: 'capitalism can not only tolerate, but even actually incite and exploit, forms of "perverse" sexuality' (Žižek 1999: 226). Nonetheless, Bourdieu does not seem to recognize in his work on gender that masculine and feminine identities are not unified configurations, but a series of uneasily sutured, potentially conflictual subject positions. In short, by failing to draw out the destabilizing implications of the notion of the field for an understanding of gender identity, Bourdieu has no conception of multiple subjectivity (Moore 1994: 80). His account of the somatization of gender relations, therefore, suggests that the symbolic formations of masculinity and femininity are unproblematically mapped onto the social realm where men unambiguously occupy the dominant position and women the subordinate one. This invariant logic of male domination and female subordination oversimplifies the complexities of gender identity in late-capitalist society and hypostatizes relations between men and women.

If the concept of the field is considered in conjunction with the idea of habitus – as Bourdieu does elsewhere in his thought – then this hypostatization is undone and the ramifications of these indissociable categories for a theory of agency begin to unfold. Following Butler, it is important to have a sense of the indeterminacies immanent to the process through which hegemonic gender norms are reproduced. However, it is also important not to conflate symbolic indeterminacy with resistance or political agency which depends on a more complex analysis of the configuration of relations of power between different social fields. It is only by considering how the indeterminacies of symbolic formations are mediated through diverse material relations that a more precise sense of political agency may be reached. Far from denying agency as Butler claims, Bourdieu's idea of the generative dynamic between habitus and field leads to a more nuanced view of political agency in terms of the idea of regulated liberties which escapes from the binary of domination–resistance in which, at some level, Butler's thought remains caught. In addition, the complex model

of power relations that the concept invokes serves as a cor-
rective to some of the sociologically naive claims about the
transformation of social and sexual identities made in recent
social theoretical work on detraditionalization.

Regulated liberties and resistance

Bourdieu's idea that opportunities for subversive misappropriation increase with the lengthening of circuits of
legitimation in late-capitalism quite closely resembles the
non-oppositional account of resistance encapsulated in Butler's
idea of the resignification of dominant norms (e.g. Bourdieu
1996: 387). In this respect, Butler's and Bourdieu's understanding of the conditions of emergence for subversive behaviour
are not that dissimilar; rather, the underlying dispute centres
on their conceptualization of political agency which is formed
around their divergent conceptions of the relation between
symbolic forms and social context.

Bourdieu does not deny the heterodox force of performative
resignifications; however, he emphasizes that these are always
situated within a particular 'field' of power relations which, in
turn, must be understood in terms of its overarching connections with other fields in the social totality. Butler's assertion
that Bourdieu rehabilitates the base–superstructure distinction
in order to reduce the symbolic to an epiphenomenon of the
social fails to recognize the refractory force of the concept of
the field (Butler 1997a: 157). The idea of the field potentially
yields a differentiated and dynamic model of power relations
where each field has its own historicity and logic which may
reinforce or conflict with those of other fields. This view, where
symbolic power is examined in terms of its connection to
other power relations, does not rob symbolic power of its autonomy, or conflate speech with effects. It does, however, produce
a more nuanced, and perhaps more cautious assessment of
political agency and the changes that can be wrought through
resignificatory practices. Bourdieu is critical of the dichotomous
logic of domination–resistance which tends to simplify the complex nature of freedom and constraint in capitalist society and

instead employs the term 'regulated liberties' to denote a
more complex relation between the dominant and its subjects
(Bourdieu 1991: 102).

The idea of 'regulated liberties' echoes the concern of Butler
and other feminist theorists to think of political agency and
change within gender norms in non-oppositional terms. Like
the notion of the hybrid in post-colonial theory, it suggests a
form of change which emerges, not as opposition or external-
ity, but as dislocation arising from the reinscription of the
tools and symbols of the dominant into the space of the
colonized (Bhabha 1994: 109). It provides a way of obviating
simplified theories of oppression and is useful for an understanding of what are perceived to be significant assertions of
women's autonomy in the last twenty years which rest on an
ambivalent relation with conventional notions and images of
femininity. For example, the tentative renegotiation of heterosexual relations beyond the institution of marriage. Or, for
example, the claims made in studies of 'girl culture' that highly
femininized cultural icons, notably Madonna, provide teenage
girls with a set of symbolic tools with which to subvert patriarchal definitions of femininity (Kaplan 1993). Or, the appropriation by 'lipstick' lesbians of the signifiers of conventional
femininity to throw into question stereotyped representations
of non-heterosexuals (Bell et al. 1994). Such changes cannot
be understood through binaries of domination and resistance,
but rather involve more complex processes of investment and
negotiation. They are illustrative of how the feminine subject
is synchronically produced as the object of regulatory norms
by phallocentric symbolic systems and formed as a subject or
agent who may resist these norms. In this view, gender identity is not a mechanistically determining structure but an open
system of dispositions – regulated liberties – that are 'durable
but not eternal' (Bourdieu 1992: 133).

Yet, like the notion of the hybrid, ideas of performative
resignification, parody, masquerade and so forth need to be
situated within a determinate material context lest they turn into
a self-identical principle that effaces the specificity of particular struggles (McClintock 1995: 61–9). As Homi Bhabha has
observed, the dominant is often shielded from the potentially

destabilizing effects of the ambivalences of (colonized) subjectivity: 'caught in the Imaginary as they are, these shifting positionalities will never seriously threaten the dominant power relations, for they exist to exercise them pleasurably and productively' (Bhabha 1983: 205). In this regard, a limitation of Butler's primarily symbolic and abstract concept of agency is that it underestimates the extent to which there can be a systemic recuperation of seemingly radical practices. The emancipatory effects of the emergence of a given subaltern identity have to be considered in the context of the structures of consumerism that have played a part in its creation and which render it susceptible to 'commodification, recuperation, and depoliticization' (Fraser 1995: 163). Nicola Field observes, for example, that many types of identity politics replace radical ideas of struggle against oppression with a reverence for lifestyle and a fetishization of the position of the marginalized consumer: 'gay lifestyle is visible as a specialised form of middle-class lifestyle and therefore is second nature to some, completely unattainable and meaningless to many' (Field 1997: 260).

The problem with the concept of resignification, and associated terms such as abjection, is that its status as a symbolic mechanism is not sufficient to analyse the 'overdetermined entanglements of discursive and non-discursive social arrangements', of symbolic, political and economic power relations that give rise to the emergence of new identities (Hennessy 1992: 86). The distinction between speech and conduct, the symbolic and the material, becomes blurred again. The symbolic comes to metonymically represent other social and political relations and Butler's idea of political agency remains, therefore, an abstract potentiality rather than the result of specific social practices. There is no doubt, for example, that the resignification of the term 'queer' has been a powerful catalyst in the emergence of set of gay identities; however, these transformations are also predicated on a complex set of socio-economic changes associated, on the most general level, with the detraditionalization of social relations in late-capitalism. It is not just a case of the resignification of dominant terms by marginal or abject groups because, in a sense, the ability of these groups to collectively institute new forms of identity suggests that their social location is not unambiguously marginal. As historians such as John D'Emilio have shown, the emergence of a metropolitan gay identity is predicated on a convergence of social and symbolic relations which tend towards the simultaneous inclusion and exclusion of homosexual groups (D'Emilio 1984). The economic centrality of the gay consumer – the 'pink pound' – has facilitated the greater visibility of a marginalized sexuality in a way that the notion of resignification does not really capture.

This is not to reassert a problematic dualism where material struggles are seen as separable and prior to symbolic ones. In her article 'Merely Cultural', Butler rightly criticizes the resurgence of an orthodox Leftism which dismisses queer politics as an epiphenomenal fixation on identity forestalling an analysis of a more fundamental politics of redistribution. Against this, Butler argues that not only is the distinction between the material and symbolic unstable, but also redistributive issues lie at the heart of a politics of cultural recognition:

> Is it possible to distinguish ... between a lack of cultural recognition and a material oppression, when the very definition of legal 'personhood' is rigorously circumscribed by cultural norms that are indissociable from their material effects? For example, in those instances in which lesbians and gays are excluded from state-sanctioned notions of the family ... stopped at the border, deemed inadmissible to citizenship. (Butler 1998: 41)

Ultimately, this assertion of a distinction between the cultural and the material has homophobic effects in that queer politics are deemed secondary and excluded from the sphere of the properly political. While Butler is right to question the opposition of the material and cultural, it is still important to attempt to distinguish analytically between the different logics of social fields if the discontinuous and uneven effects of political change are to be understood. For example, an understanding of differences between the status and political visibility of lesbian mothers and single gay men requires an examination of the variable access of these groups to cultural and economic goods. While both groups are victims of homophobic cultural sanctions, the arguably greater cultural visibility of gay men can be explained partly in terms of better access to economic and other material resources. The attempt to disentangle the different power relations that determine levels of political agency need not result in a reinvocation of a materialist reductionism or a legitimation of a hierarchy of oppressions. Rather, an analysis of the transformatory effects of resignification upon entrenched norms requires a contextualization within wider socio-economic relations and an understanding of agency not just as a structural potentiality but as a set of embedded practices.

The idea of the performative clearly alludes to the complex interplay of material and symbolic relations but does not really attempt to disaggregate them analytically. As a result, Butler's work often moves too quickly from outlining the constitutive instability of symbolic systems to claiming a political status for certain 'excentric' sexual practices (Hennessy 1992). For example, as Osborne and Segal point out, the parodic reinscription of heterosexual norms is most effective in subcultures that are predisposed to the dissolution of hegemonic identities (Osborne and Segal 1994: 38). In other contexts, the same reinscription can serve to re-idealize rather than denaturalize heterosexual norms, as Moya Lloyd observes: 'parody might be transgressive from the perspective of the specific linear history of practices that constitute a particular individuated subject . . . This does not guarantee, however, that it is parodic when seen in the context of others' (Lloyd 1999: 208). This is not to deny the challenge that the assertion of homosexual rights poses to heterosexuality. It does, however, throw into question some of the wider political claims made about individualized sexual practices which privilege one dimension of oppression over others (Bourdieu 1999: 134). It constitutes what Grosz calls 'a refusal to link sexual pleasure with the struggle for freedom, a refusal to validate sexuality in terms of a greater cause or a higher purpose' (Grosz 1994b: 153). Bourdieu's notion of habitus permits the thinking of the synchronous nature of constraint and freedom expressed in the hybrid form that women's social experience has assumed. At the same time, however, it guards against a conflation of the potentiality for autonomous action with a celebration of its subversive political significance. The fact that individuals do not straightforwardly reproduce the social system is not a guarantee of the inherently resistant nature of their actions. Bourdieu is critical of the tendency to 'spontaneist populism' that haunts certain forms of cultural studies (e.g. Fiske 1989). He claims that practices often hailed as 'resistant' may have an impact only on the relatively superficial 'effective' relations of a field rather than its deeper structural relations (1992: 113).

Affect and interest

Bourdieu's article 'On the Family as a Realized Category' (1996) provides an interesting attempt to analyse the ambivalent relations that exist between symbolically constructed dynamics of affect and material interests. The family is understood as a 'collective principle of construction of collective reality', that is, as a constitutive element within the habitus. It is both an objective and a subjective social category which plays a funda-mental role in the ordering of social practice and the perception of experience. As a tacitly internalized principle of perception, the family endows experience with a commonsensical or self-evident appearance, that is, the family appears as the most natural of social categories. Thus, the family is both an im-manent and a transcendent structure: '[it] is both immanent in individuals (as an internalized collective) and transcendent to them, since they encounter it in the form of objectivity in all other relations' (1996: 21).

The functionalist aspects to Bourdieu's analysis of the family are familiar from sociological and anthropological literature and, indeed, from his earlier work (e.g. Bourdieu and Passeron 1977). The structure of the family and its legitimacy is deter-mined by the role it plays in the accumulation and transmis-sion of economic, cultural and symbolic privileges, such as property, the family name and social capital. It is through this labour of institutionalization that integrative forces are mobilized against fragmenting social tendencies, rendering the family a relatively enduring social unit. Of more interest is Bourdieu's analysis of the internal emotional logic of the field in terms of the symbolical inculcation of obliged affections and of affective obligations of family feeling. The family is characterized by a constant and intense maintenance work which turns the nominal bonds of the family group ('she's your sister...') into profoundly uniting affective bonds. Through a ceaseless practical and symbolic labour comprising a myriad of ordinary and continuous exchanges – exchange of gifts, service, help, attention, visits – the 'obligation to love' is transformed into a 'loving disposition' that tends to endow each member with family feeling and generates solidarity. This emotional labour of integration is especially important in that it runs against the potentially disintegrative effects of struggle over other power relations both within and beyond the field of the family.

Bourdieu's analysis of the realization of affective relations within the family represents a significant refinement of his own understanding of agency. Elsewhere in his work, Bourdieu argues that actors are motivated by a struggle over specific goods or capital within a given field and, even when appearing to occupy a radical or heterodox position, they still hold an investment in the underlying *illusio* or rules of the game. Many commentators have rightly criticized this view of the motivations of social actors as being not dissimilar to rational action theory in its emphasis on strategic and instrumental orientation (e.g. Calhoun 1983: 70–1). Certainly, such a model of the underlying logic that operates in a given field does not seem appropriate to analyse forms of social interaction – such as familial and other intimate relations – that are overlaid with affective and altruistic bonds. In his essay on the family, albeit elliptical, Bourdieu suggests that affectual motivations have an ambivalent relation with the material instrumental interests of actors, sometimes reinforcing them, sometimes running counter to them. Thus, although the family is one of the primary sites where individuals are accommodated to the social system, the bonds that it generates are always in excess of any socializing function. Against determinist analyses, the family is seen, therefore, as internally contradictory: 'it does not form its own dynamic, nor is it part of the dynamic of capitalist production' (German 1997: 153). It is such contradictions that are generative of agency.

Bourdieu does not pursue the implications of this ambivalent relation between the affectual and the material for an understanding of agency in gender relations; they can be inferred from other feminist work in this area. Nancy Fraser, for example, criticizes the tendency within certain feminist work to explain gender inequalities solely with reference to a symbolic logic of subordination. In particular, Fraser focuses on Carole Pateman's argument in *The Sexual Contract* where she uses the master–slave dynamic to explain how gender inequalities are established in familial relations. Fraser criticizes the explanatory force that this symbolic dynamic is invested with because, in her view, it obscures the analysis of structural or systemic processes that undergird hierarchical social relations. For example, within marriage, power has less to do with an implicit sexual contract and 'male sex right' and more to do with the ability to exit which is defined by structural factors such as inferior labour market opportunities and child-care demands. Furthermore, whereas these structural asymmetries may reinforce inequalities within the marriage contract, equally the mediation of the marriage contract through systemic and non-congruent relations may create the potential for trade-offs and new forms of autonomy:

> even as the wage contract establishes the worker as subject to the boss's command in the employment sphere, it simultaneously constitutes that sphere as a limited sphere. 'The outside' here includes both a market in consumer commodities into which the wage buys entry and a noncommodified domestic sphere in which much of the work of social reproduction is performed without pay by women. In those arenas, which are themselves permeated by power and inequality, the wage functions as a resource and a source of leverage. For some women, it buys a reduction in vulnerability through marriage. (Fraser 1997: 230)

In short, the realization of patterns of autonomy and dependence within gender relations cannot be fully captured in symbolic dyads of master–slave, the normal–deviant because power often resides in impersonal structural mechanisms that are lived through more ambiguous cultural forms.

Ultimately, then, the emphasis in the negative paradigm on the symbolic determination of the subject yields a fairly one-dimensional account of agency which does not sufficiently consider other abstract forms of social mediation. A more active notion of agency emerges, however, once its key role in the mediation of symbolic and material relations is understood. In other words, by conceptualizing the relation between the material and symbolic as generative of variable patterns of autonomy and dependence then a more determinate sense of agency emerges. As we shall see in the next section, this has destabilizing implications for certain work on detraditionalization whose deployment of a problematic notion of reflexive agency as a uniform effect of post-conventional societies is also underpinned by an undifferentiated symbolic logic. This results in a rather naive view of the expressive possibilities offered within late-capitalist societies and, in particular, of the potential for transformation in gender relations.

Cathexis and reflexivity

Certain theories of detraditionalization connect the emergence of heightened levels of reflexive self-awareness to tendencies within late-capitalist societies towards the aestheticization and dedifferentiation of experience. This process of dedifferentiation involves both the intensification and destabilization of symbolic images. A symbolic logic, paradigmatically expressed in the image, comes to permeate all areas of social practice and, as a result of this saturation, any straightforward referential relation between image and reality is destabilized. Although such theories are suggestive, they are ultimately limited by the priority accorded to the over-generalized idea of aesthetization which forecloses an analysis of the specificity of the power relations in which a reflexive management of the self is ineluctably embedded. The idea of aesthetic dedifferentiation leads, in turn, to an implicit reinstalling of a disembodied, disembedded self who moves freely across the social realm. In contrast, the situating of agency within the specific dynamics that operate across and within fields links the emergence of reflexivity to a determinate context. The embodied potentialities of the habitus are only ever realized in the context of a specific field and, therefore, rather than being a generalized capacity, reflexivity is understood as a variable effect dependent on a particular configuration of power relations. Such a notion makes it possible to conceptualize any changes within gender identity as uneven and discontinuous.

It is in the work of thinkers such as Scott Lash (1990), Mike Featherstone (1992) and Michel Maffesoli (1988) that the idea of identity transformation is conceived of primarily as an aesthetic process. The notion of aesthetic reflexivity is partly taken from Foucault's notion of an aesthetics of existence as a form of ethical labour on the self that challenges what are held to be the self-evident, natural elements of identity. It is also derived from Baudrillard's (1983) argument that late-capitalist society is increasingly dominated by a referentless symbolic logic that leads to a dedifferentiation of the distinct spheres of activity and thought characteristic of the era of high modernity. For Baudrillard, these associated notions of aestheticization, hyperreality and social implosion result in a nihilistic vision of an apolitical, indifferent mass society. Lash and Featherstone give these ideas a positive inflection by combining them with Foucault's work on the self, thereby emphasizing the expressive possibilities generated by the tendencies towards dedifferentiation. Lash claims, for example, that the movement towards aestheticization leads to a dedifferentiation of the socio-cultural sphere instituting a postmodern regime of 'figural signification'. The intrusion of a figural aesthetics into the lifeworld problematizes social experience by drawing attention to its constructed nature. This has destabilizing and potentially emancipatory effects upon traditional systems of representation and, in particular, upon hegemonic constructions of collective and individual identity.

A problem with such arguments about the expressive possibilities generated by processes of aesthetic dedifferentiation is that they are based primarily on a generalized symbolic logic

of cathexis and identification which does not adequately explain the emergence of reflexive self-awareness. The transformation of identity is predicated on a moment of instantiation
or identity between subject and symbolic structure. Postmodern
figural sensibility operates not through meaning, as does the
discursive sensibility of modernity, but through direct impact.
It is a visual rather than a literary sensibility that is non-
rational, non-hierarchical and operates through direct instantiation or the unmediated investment of the spectator's desire
in the cultural object (Lash 1990: 175). Michel Maffesoli's
(1988) argument for the emergence of a mass 'ethic of aesthetics'
presumes a similar logic of identification embedded in postmodern patterns of consumption.

Such a logic of cathetic identification cannot fully sustain
the idea of reflexivity because cathexis is a dynamic force or
psychic energy which exists prior to any critical horizon
(Laplanche and Pontalis 1973: 62–5). A critical understanding
of the process of identity formation cannot arise, therefore,
from the direct instantiation of the subject with symbolic structures (cf. Ricoeur 1981). The assumption of a direct identification is problematic in so far as it invokes an absolute submission
on the part of the subject 'who would passively incorporate all
the determinations of the object' (Laclau 1994: 14). Furthermore, the use of the notion of cathexis to characterize the
ways in which individuals identify with symbolic objects does
not adequately distinguish between the different modalities
this relation may assume. Niklas Luhmann, for example, dis-
tinguishes between cognitive and normative modes of identification; the former being disposed towards learning
whereas the latter is not (Luhmann 1995: 320–1). Reflexive
self-knowledge would straddle the two modalities in so far as it
is not possible to establish an absolute separation between them.
However, reflexivity in the sense of a self-conscious shaping
of identity would presumably involve a greater degree of cognitive expectation and the notion of direct instantiation fails
to signal this. This is not to confine political action to an intentionalist paradigm, or to deny that important and unanticipated
political effects may emerge from affectual dynamics. Indeed,
this is one of the insights of Butler's notion of performative

resignification that subversion is 'the kind of effect that *resists calculation*' (1993b: 29). Nonetheless, to insist on the inevitability of incalculability is to celebrate a form of spontaneism and to fetishize the inchoate, leaving unexplained the range and political force of many other types of cultural action.

If agency is not to be reified in a form of spontaneism, then reflexivity must be understood as emerging, at least in part, from the distantiation provoked by the conflict and tension of social forces operating within and across specific fields. It is not an evenly generalized capacity of subjects living in a detraditionalized era, but arises unevenly from their embeddedness within differing sets of power relations. This suggests that any shifts in gender norms cannot unilaterally be attributed to a non-specific process of aesthetic destabilization. An indeterminacy which forms the ontological grounds for the emergence of change becomes elided with the emancipatory or political *per se*. Echoing problems in Butler's thought, resistance becomes an inevitable consequence of instability rather than a potentiality whose realization is contingent upon a certain configuration of power relations (McNay 1996). Lash's arguments, for example, rest on a short-circuited movement from the ontological to the political. He argues that 'gender bending' in adverts problematizes reality and the normative through the deliberate ambiguity in gender and sexual preference that is built into such images. The effect of this symbolic problematization is an opening up of social identities to produce a 'more ambivalent and less fixed positioning of subjectivity' (1990: 198). The problem with such an argument is that it elides a dynamics of symbolic destabilization with processes of social and political transformation. A consideration of gender shows that whilst there may have been a loosening of dominant images of femininity, the transformatory impact of these images upon women's social status is far from certain (e.g. Walby 1992). As Walby observes, hegemonic norms of femininity are no longer exclusively centred around a constricting association of women with the domestic sphere. In their place, more diverse and public images of women have emerged. However, these new norms are saturated by an ideology of the perpetual sexual availability of women for men. Rather than being self-evidently emancipatory, the destabilization of images of femininity may be indicative of more insidious forms of subordination captured by Walby in the idea of the shift from private to public patriarchy (Walby 1990: 107). In short, by conflating symbolic ambivalence with social detraditionalization, some theories of reflexive transformation overestimate the significance and the extent of the expressive possibilities available to men and women in late-capitalist society.

If there can be said to have been any attenuation of conventional notions of masculinity and femininity in the last thirty years or so, it needs to be thought of as a much more piecemeal, discontinuous affair reflecting, in part, the negotiation of complex relations of power by individuals in their movement within and across fields of social action. For example, women entering the workforce after child-rearing may experience difficulties because their expectations and predispositions constituted largely through the exigencies of the domestic field sit uneasily with the objective requirements of the workplace. At the same time, this dissonance may lead to a greater awareness – what Bourdieu calls the 'lucidity of the excluded' – of the shortcomings of a system of employment based on gender discrimination. In other words, reflexive awareness is predicated on a distantiation of the subject from constitutive structures. The questioning of conventional notions of femininity does not arise just from exposure to and identification with a greater array of alternative images of femininity, but from tensions inherent in the concrete negotiation of increasingly conflictual female roles. Such a process is suggested in Teresa De Lauretis's work on gendered identity as both the effect of representation and that which remains beyond representation – that is, the cross-cutting and conflictual practices of self-representation (De Lauretis 1987). Furthermore, the often implicit equation of reflexive self-awareness with post-conventional modes of behaviour needs to be scrutinized (Thompson 1996). If the idea of reflexive agency is to have relevance for an understanding of the ways in which gender relations may be undergoing restructuring, it must be qualified with a differentiated analysis of attendant social relations and with a more circumscribed account of reflexive agency as an unevenly realized phenomenon.

Beyond the public and private

The emphasis placed on reflexive agency as a variable effect emerging from the mediation of symbolic and material relations suggests an uneven pattern of change in gender relations which cannot be understood fully in analytical dyads. The public–private distinction is one such dualism which much feminist theory has focused on unpacking because of the extent to which it underplays the differentiated nature of social life by confining a notion of women's agency to the domestic sphere. The social realization of gender relations cannot be properly understood as being mapped onto a straightforward division between the public and private, not least because the relationship between the two realms has become more complex in late-modernity (e.g. Offe 1987). Yet, despite the force of such critiques, this dualism is often perpetuated at a tacit level in feminist work on gender identity. Anna Yeatman (1984), for example, argues that in their recovery of domestic life, many feminists accept implicitly the logic that renders the distinction between the domestic and the public as an opposition between the social and the extra-social rather than as a differentiation between two forms of sociality. A consequent assumption emerges that public sociality is the paradigm of social life and the residual status of the domestic is assured. This is evident, for example, in Dorothy Smith's (1987) work which, despite recognizing the extent to which the domestic is traversed by other power relations, proceeds to hermetically seal it off in order to sustain a cohesive notion of a feminine standpoint.[5] Although it is explicitly anti-dualist, Butler's pre-eminently symbolic formulation of performative politics ultimately also does little to dislodge the private–public dichotomy.

To overcome such dichotomies, it is necessary to develop further an understanding of the internally differentiated nature of gender relations through a mapping of the imbrication of material and symbolic forms. Bourdieu's emphasis on the autonomous logic of each field suggests a way of conceptualizing this differentiation within gender relations: 'there are as many

ways of realizing femininity as there are classes and class frac-
tions' (1979: 107–8). The dissonance outlined between the
subjective dispositions and objective relations embedded within
the field of the family can be taken further than Bourdieu's
elusive remarks in order to examine the ways in which contemporary gender relations may be undergoing a process of
restructuring in other realms. For example, while intimate relations – particularly parent–child relations – are predominantly
reproduced within the domestic sphere, it is no longer the
exclusive site of the reproduction of these relations. Intimate
relations may be understood as becoming increasingly un-
bounded and having variable effects across different fields. For
example, the separation of the domestic from the intimate
permits a consideration of possible changes in gender relations
emerging from what is seen to be the new centrality of intimacy to conventionally more impersonal fields of social action.
Luhmann (1986) argues that the demand for intensive, intimate
relations traditionally confined to the female domestic arena
has spilled over into other areas of social life (also Beck and
Beck-Gernsheim 1995). The effects of this new centrality of
the intimate are contested. On the one hand, it is associated
with a regression of the public sphere and a fetishization of
the self (Foucault 1978; Sennett 1976). On the other hand, it
could be seen as potentially emancipatory in that it is no longer
exclusively women who are burdened with the responsibility
for emotional well-being. As Francesca Cancian suggests, it
may even be liberating for women to enter into certain types
of instrumental relations more usually associated with interaction between men (Cancian 1989).

In sum, as a relational concept the field yields an understanding of society as a differentiated and open structure the
negotiation of which yields an active and determinate idea of
agency beyond that of generalized notions of reflexivity or the
performative. This in turn provides a framework in which to
conceptualize the uneven and non-systematic ways in which
subordination and autonomy are realized in women's lives. By
construing intimate and domestic relations as overlapping but
distinct fields of behaviour, their interconnection and relations
with other fields of sociality can be thought not as implacable

opposition but in terms of multiple disjunction, overlap and conflict.

Conclusion

Against criticisms of the determinist tendencies of his work, I have argued that Bourdieu's work sketches out more fully than a Foucauldian constructionism how the autonomous subject emerges from constraint. His work begins to move from a determinist to a generative understanding of subjectification and agency in two respects. First, Bourdieu counterbalances the uni-directional notion of temporality – understood as the sedimented effects of exogenous power systems upon the body – deployed in much constructionist work with a consideration of the praxeological implications of embodiment for an idea of agency. In other words, a model of discursive determination is replaced by a more dialogical, temporal logic. Second, the couplet of habitus–field permits Bourdieu to link the symbolic process whereby the body is invested with meaning to surrounding material relations. Although these connections are often implied in constructionist work, they cannot be fully explored because of the lack of an active concept of agency. As a result, agency is considered within the confined parameters of the indeterminacy of meaning systems. This is paralleled, in feminist theory, by the narrowing of the issue of the social construction of gender to that of sexuality. Bourdieu extends the idea of symbolic inscription by placing it in the context of the material relations of the field. This suggests a complex dynamic between the symbolic and the material, where the logic of the field may reinforce or displace the tendencies of the habitus. It is this tension that is generative of agency.

A limitation in Bourdieu's account of the logic of practice is that it lacks a developed theory of multiple subjectivity. His work concentrates on the implications of power and position for a theory of agency, but it tends to disregard the internally complex nature of subjectivity and how this is worked through at the level of motivation and self-understanding. It is the insights generated for a theory of agency by a hermeneutic perspective on self-formation which will be considered in the next chapter. Highlighting the active role played by the subject in the construction of a coherent identity allows a more nuanced concept of agency to emerge. A dynamic account of the process of self-formation also mediates the antinomy of stasis and change which dominates much thought on identity.

3

GENDER AND NARRATIVE: RICOEUR ON THE COHERENCE OF THE SELF

Introduction

The issue of the identity of the self, in particular, the question of its coherence, is one that has been relatively neglected in the poststructural emphasis on the contradictory and dispersed nature of subjectivity. It is by incorporating an explanation of the ways in which coherent notions of selfhood are maintained into an account of subject formation that an active dimension of agency is unfolded. The idea that a coherent sense of self is a necessary dimension of subject formation suggests that there are limits to the way in which subjectivity may be transformed. This modifies the rather unqualified idea of the contingency of the subject, often presumed in the negative paradigm, which may result in naive accounts of the extent to which identities are amenable to refashioning.

Paul Ricoeur's conception of the narrative structure of the self suggests a dynamic or creative substrate to agency. Moreover, the temporalized understanding of the self that the idea of narrative captures – that is, the self has unity, but it is the dynamic unity of change through time – goes some way to overcoming certain oppositions around which much thought on identity tends to revolve, notably the dualism of essential (stasis) versus constructed (change) concepts of identity and that of authentic experience versus ideological distortion. It also indicates a revised approach to the often overstated rejection of the category of identity and consequent endorsement of a politics of non-identity that is prevalent in certain types of feminist and poststructural theory. Against this separation of identity from non-identity, it suggests that the two are inextricably intertwined in the moment of distantiation that underlies any assertion of the self. Finally, the idea of temporal complexity at the heart of narrative identity offers one way of conceptualizing the mediated nature of gender in late-capitalist societies.

Identity of the self

The issue of personal or self-identity – that is, the process through which individuals are routinely and actively involved in the meaningful interpretation of the self in social interaction – is one that is relatively under-theorized in poststructural thought. This is partly a result of the emphasis in poststructural thought on the fragmented nature of subjectivity which tends to dissolve any notion of the coherent self and results in what Ernesto Laclau and Chantal Mouffe have famously called an 'essentialism of the elements' where the connections between the multiple subject positions constitutive of individuality remain unthought (Laclau and Mouffe 1985: 116). The degree of emphasis on the essential fragmentation and dispersal of subjectivity varies between different poststructuralist thinkers: from Baudrillard's celebration of the schizoid as the paradigm of subjectivity, through the Lacanian stress on the lack that perpetually disrupts the illusion of symbolic unity, to Foucault's idea that identity is a socially specific phenomenon constructed through the interplay of technologies of domination and practices of the self. Despite these differences, the general orientation of poststructural theory is towards demonstrating the constitution of a fragile subjectivity within contradiction, conflict and exclusion. The burden of such theories is not towards explaining how, despite the dispersed nature of subjectivity, individuals are able to act autonomously. This presumes at some level an ability to maintain a unified conception of self. This is a particular weakness in poststructural accounts of subjectification because, as Laclau and Mouffe put it: 'analysis cannot simply remain at the moment of dispersion, given that "human identity" involves not merely an ensemble of dispersed positions but also forms of overdetermination existing among them' (1985: 117).

There are several difficulties associated with the dispersion model of subject formation, not least, as feminists have frequently pointed out, that it deprives emancipatory theory of any concept of subjectivity through which the experiences of marginalized groups can be recovered and politicized (e.g. Lovibond 1989: 28–9). Another difficulty is that the emphasis on dispersion leads to a concept of the coherence of self as an imposed illusion or discursive effect. In other words, the idea of subjectification is essentially a negative one where all identity becomes an externally imposed effect. Paradoxically, this is evident in the work of Laclau and Mouffe who, despite recognizing the problems arising from an interminable dispersion of the subject, solve the issue through reference to a process of symbolic overdetermination (Laclau and Mouffe 1985: 118). Without being qualified with a more active notion of self-formation, the unsupported idea of overdetermination remains within a negative paradigm of subject formation as imposition which renders the agent little more than a 'place-filler, a recipient of . . . directives which issue from some other, heteronomous source of authority, and which cannot be conceived as in any way belonging to a project of autonomous self-creation' (Norris 1993: 33). Ideological formations undoubtedly play a determining role in the construction of a unified subjectivity, but Laclau and Mouffe tend to disregard the ways in which this may be accompanied by a more active process of self-interpretation on the part of the subject. The active role played by the subject in the process of identity formation is captured in hermeneutics, for example, through the notion of the 'pre-interpreted' nature of social life. This denotes the idea that individuals do not passively absorb external determinations, but are actively engaged in the interpretation of experience and, therefore, in a process of self-formation, albeit on a pre-reflexive level.

With regard to gender identity, the hermeneutic idea of the pre-interpreted nature of experience provides a way of considering how the ambiguities of the process through which the individual appropriates gender norms are worked through at the level of self-identity. How it may be, for example, that, despite the compulsory nature of heterosexual norms, there seems to be a lack of correspondence between these norms and individual practices. The connection between hegemonic norms and the persistence of gender hierarchies, while powerful, is not to be understood as one of reflection; symbolic codes are not transmitted in any straightforward way into individual practice. The one-sided nature of certain constructionist accounts of subject formation does not capture these ambiguities sufficiently; it does not explain adequately how individuals may be attached to their subjugation, or the investments, conscious or otherwise, that individuals may hold in deeply irrational and oppressive gender identities (Holloway 1984).

A latent violence informs uni-directional models of subjectification which disallows the elaboration of a more substantive model of agency, by reducing subjectivity to a substrate of force (e.g. Rose 1984: 178–80). While there may be an element of violence inherent to the assertion of identity, this dynamic is not exhaustive of all aspects of subject formation; in particular, it cannot capture the active role played by the subject in self-formation. As Hans Joas puts it: 'identity formation can only succeed under dialogical conditions; violence and exclusion may serve to *stabilize* identities and to this extent are functional equivalents of dialogical stabilization, but are not on their own able to serve as the basis for identity *formation*' (Joas 1998: 15). The negative paradigm not only diminishes the subject to the status of a passive recipient of external determinations, but it also results in an elliptical understanding of agency.

A consequence of the one-sided idea of subject formation as a process of imposition is that an exclusionary dynamic vis-à-vis connection to the other is privileged. The stabilization of identity is understood as being achieved through a process of exclusion of the other or denial of difference. Identity is asserted through the rejection of any form of difference that is

unsettling to the self. Difficulties arise with this exclusionary
dynamic when it is offered as an exhaustive explanation of all
dimensions of subjectification because it says little substantive
about the range of possible responses of an actor faced with
social complexity, contradiction and alterity. Different modes
of relating to the other in a meaningful way – for example, the
ability to accept connectedness to the other or the capacity for
reconciliation – are foreclosed. In short, the idea of agency that
stems from this partial idea of subject formation remains within
the primarily negative terms of resistance, disidentification or
subversion of dominant norms and fails to 'theorize non-
oppositional and non-dominating relations' (Weir 1996: 4).
The ability of the subject to respond to difference openly, to
respond creatively to contradiction, to act in an innovative
fashion and so forth may be implied, but can only be asserted
rather than derived from such a negative account. Given that
exclusion is the condition of possibility of all identities and
that not all identities are oppressive, there is a need to demon-
strate how a coherent sense of self is not exclusively maintained through a suppression of difference and otherness. The
failure in much work on identity to supplement the negative,
exclusionary account of subject formation means, in the final
analysis, that ideas of agency remain caught inevitably within
the impoverished dualisms of domination and resistance, identification and disidentification.

Time and the self

Temporalizing an understanding of subjectification makes it
possible to move beyond the negative paradigm in order to
think through some of the questions raised by the issue of
self-identity for a theory of agency. A temporal understanding
of the construction of self-identity offers a way of explaining
such phenomena as the historical embeddedness of certain
gender norms and also the way in which contradictions within
configurations of the self are mediated. The relative failure of
poststructural theory to conceptualize the temporal dimensions
of identity often results in aporetic accounts of subjectivity as

either fragmented and in flux (e.g. Baudrillard's schizoid) or as inexorably shaped by normalizing social forces (e.g. Foucault's 'docile body'). The tendency to rely on atemporal conceptions of identity has been exacerbated by the falsely polarizing effects of the debate over essentialism. In general, thought on identity has often become stranded in sterile antinomy between so-called essentialist concepts and a post-Nietzschean constructivism of which both concepts are fundamentally ahistorical. On the one hand, as a result of overuse, the term essentialism lacks analytical precision and tends to conflate all attempts to think of the coherence of the self with efforts to impute an unchanging core to identity. On the other side, the social constructionist account of the subject as a contingent formation lacks historical depth and is unable to explain the durability of certain forms of identity. In short, the poststructural account of identity is temporally underdeveloped and cannot explain why certain forms of gendered behaviour endure long after the historical circumstances in which they emerge have faded.

In an attempt to avoid such aporia, recent feminist work on gender has begun to unpack aspects of the relation between subjectification and time. Materialist feminism has tended to focus on the centrality of macrostructural concepts of time to an analysis of change and diversity in gender relations, for example, as macro-changes in overarching gender regimes, as the convergence of time and space expressed in the sedimentation of institutional practices or as the intersection of different forms of time and the way in which these impact upon the lives of individuals (Walby 1997: 8–12, cf. Saltzman Chafetz 1990). The weakness of this work is that it often lacks a concept of agency through which to examine the effects of such macrostructural tendencies upon the lives of individuals. In the previous chapter, we saw how feminist work on embodiment attempts to elaborate a more dialogical notion of temporality in order to conceptualize the emergence of agency from constraint. Rather than thinking of gender as a quasi-permanent structure, it is thought of as a temporally regulated constellation of socio-symbolic norms and practices. Linear models of time as a series of punctuated instances are replaced by an ostensibly more dialogical conception in which the constraints of social structures are reproduced, and also partially transcended, in the practices of agents. The individual's transcendence of the immediacy of the present through encounter with unforeseen events opens up a space of variability and potential change within gender norms. Despite the insights generated in this work, it still tends to offer a symbolic account of the conditions of possibility of agency rather than a more determinate notion of agency and a more specific explanation of the dynamics of self-formation.

In order to avoid an absolutization of the subject, any theory of agency must be placed within the context of overarching material and symbolic constraints. However, at the same time, these determinist tendencies need to be counterbalanced by a hermeneutic understanding of the process of self-formation. The concept of narrative has a key role in mediating this tension between determinist and hermeneutic conceptions of agency. The understanding of narrative as foundational to the construction of a coherent sense of self within time suggests a way beyond the antinomies of dispersion versus unity, contingency versus fixity and determinism versus voluntarism around which thought on subjectification and agency often revolves. The idea of narrative shares the poststructural emphasis on the constructed nature of identity; there is nothing inevitable or fixed about the types of narrative coherence that may emerge from the flux of events. Yet, at the same time, the centrality of narrative to a sense of self suggests that there are powerful constraints or limits to the ways in which identity may be changed. Unlike the poststructural account of constraint as an exogenously imposed force, the notion of narrative indicates that constraints are imposed from without and are also self-imposed. Individuals act in certain ways because it would violate their sense of being to do otherwise. This suggests a more cautious alternative to certain claims made about the transformability of identity which often fixate on problematic ideas of indeterminacy and inchoation. In short, a certain understanding of the narrative construction of self-identity underpins an account of the active, creative dimensions of agency without falling into the attendant difficulty of voluntarism.

Narrative in feminist theory

The focus on the narrative dimensions of subjective identity is, of course, not new; many critics have commented on the constitutive role it plays in the construction of social life. As Barthes put it: 'narrative is international, transhistorical, transcultural: it is simply there, like life itself' (Barthes 1982: 251–2). The implications of an understanding of social action in terms of foundational narrative structures have been widely discussed in history and cultural and literary studies.[1] In social theory, however, it is a relatively underelaborated concept (see Carr 1985; Polkinghorne 1988; Somers and Gibson 1994). This neglect arises in part from the conceptualization of narrative in the social sciences as a particularist and non-objective mode of representation, rather than as the 'ontological' grounds of social action: 'it is through narrativity that we come to know, understand, and make sense of the social world, and . . . that we constitute our social identities (Somers and Gibson 1994: 58–9). From a positivist perspective, narrative is 'the epistemological other', a value-laden and partial mode that obscures the objective explanation of the causes of human action (Somers and Gibson 1994: 39).[2] The concept of narrative enters into macrosociological perspectives in accounts of the construction of social identity as a process of normalization or individualization. The weakness of such accounts – evident, for example, in the work of Parsons or Althusser – is that they are based on top-heavy and often ahistorical sociological categories which associate individualization with objective processes of differentiation and individuation and disregard the hermeneutic dimensions of subjectivity (Beck 1992: 128). Individuals do not construe their self-identity in terms of fixed categories, 'by assigning a predicate to the subject I' (Polkinghorne 1988: 152). The act of self-narration is central to identity formation; experience is organized along the temporal dimension, in the form of a plot that gathers events together into a coherent and meaningful structure which, in turn, gives significance to the overall configuration that is the person. Identity understood only in terms of objective social categories cannot adequately account for the lived, dynamic aspects of self-identity and may result, therefore, in reductive and reified understandings.

The concept of narrative has been central also to the feminist critique of objectivist accounts of individualization as not only determinist, but also as tacitly reproducing a masculinist view of the world. In this feminist critique, narrative becomes a central deconstructive tool because a cluster of issues associated with gender and sexuality are regarded as particularly amenable to narration (Plummer 1995). From an interpretative perspective, women's personal narratives are primary documents for feminist research because they reveal the 'reality of life' that defies or runs counter to patriarchal norms (Barbre and Personal Narratives Group 1989). Dorothy Smith, for example, has argued that a reconstruction of the 'primary narratives' of women's social practice offers a radical critique of the 'ideological narratives' of objectivity and rationality that permeate patriarchal knowledge. In a similar fashion, Patrizia Violi (1992) argues that dominant social narratives only permit the articulation of masculine forms of subjectivity. Narrative presents a trans-individual, but implicitly masculine, space which enables the elision of male identity with the collective, thereby endowing male subjects with a sense of belonging to the historical time of society. Women are excluded from these narratives and this gives rise to an 'exclusive' feminine subjectivity that is 'deeply rooted in the particularity of its own story' (Violi 1992: 173). If women's experiences are to be meaningfully symbolized, at a more general level, then the objectifying and exclusionary mode of narrative structures must be transformed. In short, an insistence on the non-correspondence between dominant social narratives and the narratives of individual lives lies at the base of the powerful feminist critique of the implicitly masculine perspective of objective modes of thought (e.g. Lara 1998; Stanley and Wise 1993).

From a structural perspective, there has been much feminist analysis of narrative in terms of the way women are brought to identify with the objectified feminine position of patriarchal symbolism; in Teresa De Lauretis's words: 'narrativity overdetermines identification' (1984: 9). In her influential *Alice Doesn't*, De Lauretis focuses on the way in which narrative operates with regard to female spectatorship. Narrative is the central instrument through which values and goals are inscribed into situational structures of meaning and through which conflicting claims of imaginary and real are mediated, arbitrated and resolved. With regard to gender identity, narrative mobilizes and articulates desires and fantasy around the roles of mythical masculine subject and feminine mythical obstacle. Women are seduced into identifying with the feminine position through the narrative generation of a surplus or 'excess' of pleasure. The positioning of the female subject in narration involves a potentially conflictual double identification with, on the one hand, the masculine gaze of the spectator and, on the other, the female object of the gaze. The potential conflict is overcome through identification with the figure of narrative movement and narrative closure. By anchoring the subject in the flow of the film's movement, the potential incommensurability of the split identification between gaze and image is overcome.

Although it is central to the analysis both of the marginalized experiences of women and of the construction of heterosexual desire, there seems to be little connection between the interpretative and structural senses of narrative invoked in this feminist work. A dichotomized understanding of the concept of narrative emerges where it is regarded as either a mode of imposing patriarchal order or as a repository of authentic knowledge. Such a dichotomy tacitly replays one of the antinomies of the debate on essentialism, namely the authentic versus the constructed nature of experience. Microsociological work on personal narratives often invokes a problematic separatism evident, for example, in Violi's claim that, because of the exclusionary nature of symbolic forms, women are confined to a particularist mode of self-understanding and 'the generalisation of individual subjectivity does not take place' (Violi 1992: 172). The difficulty with this isolationist model is that it oversimplifies the complexities of gender experience in a differentiated society in which women are increasingly involved in practices from which they have been previously excluded. It also assumes a close correspondence between the symbolic ideal of masculinity and the concrete practices of men which recent work on masculinities has shed doubt on (Garber 1992; Silverman 1992). If women's narratives are always placed at the margins of sociality, an analysis of the socio-historical dynamics through which feminine gender identity is both included and excluded from mainstream social experience is foreclosed. The stress on marginality obscures the extent to which narratives of female identity are caught up in a complex fashion with more general categories of self, personhood and history (Gilmore 1994: 13; Riley 1988).

Conversely, a difficulty with the structural feminist use of narrative is that the construction of desire is analysed in terms of the location of the subject within symbolic systems and often lacks a hermeneutic or interpretative dimension. De Lauretis emphasizes the extent to which narratives of desire are intertwined with other social practices and with extratextual codes which are non-specific to the particular form and matter of expression of the iconic sign. It is in the negotiation of these incommensurable codes that agency is situated. Nonetheless, there is little understanding of the specific mechanisms and modalities of agency, of how individuals interweave these dif- fering narrative strands. Agency is hinted at through the idea of cross-cutting identifications but is not explained, in a more active sense, as a process of self-formation. As a result, the structuralist emphasis on the construction of desire tends to efface the social aspects to the formation of the gendered sub- ject by reducing them to the dimension of sexuality (Hennessy 1992). The emphasis placed on the uni-directional process of the positioning of subjects within an invariant Oedipal nar- rative tacitly undercuts the idea of agency. Thus, when De Lauretis concludes that narratives of desire need to be sub- verted and rewritten by women, she overlooks the many other stories that have emerged despite patriarchal constraints, as Maria Pia Lara puts it: 'the fact that women have written critical and influential works of art (and philosophy, and social science) over the last century has shown that we do not need to enter an "Oedipal tale" to make a woman's life story mean- ingful' (Lara 1998: 16).

In short, structural and interpretative feminist perspectives share a representational conception of narrative which perpetuates the false antithesis of narrative as either 'a mode of imposing order on reality or as a way of unleashing a healthy disorder' (Mitchell 1980: 3). Yet, underlying such apparent antinomies, representational concepts tacitly share the view that narrative is an exogenous schema or simply one mode amongst many of imposing order upon the chaos of experience. This contrasts with Ricoeur's ontological concept of narrative as foundational in the construction of self-identity through time. As the privileged medium through which the inherent temporality of being is expressed, narrative simultaneously gives shape to identity and is the means through which selfhood is expressed. In other words, narrative is regarded not as determining but as generative of a form of self-identity which itself is neither freely willed nor externally imposed. This idea of the narrative dimensions of subject formation offers a fuller account of the creative and autonomous aspects of agency. It also helps to throw new light on the oppositions between essentialism versus constructivism and the ideological versus the authentic around which theories of gender subjectification often revolve.

Ricoeur on narrative

The category of narrative identity emerges in Ricoeur's work during the 1980s, namely the three volumes of *Time and Narrative*, the collection of essays in *From Text to Action* and, most recently, *Oneself as Another*. For Ricoeur, narrative is the fundamental category through which the aporia of temporality (such as the disjunction between cosmological and phenomenological time) are thought and is, therefore, central to the construction of social and individual identity. Narrative is a universal feature of social life; it is the fundamental mode through which the grounding of human experience in time is understood. The temporality of the human condition cannot be spoken of in direct discourse of the phenomenon, but must be mediated through the indirect discourse of narration. There is a radical inherence, but also mutual incompatibility, between constituting temporality or 'being in time' that is the condition of possibility of human experience and the lived experience of phenomenological time. Yet, at the same time, these two temporal dimensions are incommensurable. Narrative attempts to bridge this incompatibility through the construction of a third time that interweaves fiction and history; however, its failure to do so results in the multiplication of temporal aporia (Ricoeur 1988: 241).[3]

As the primary medium in which temporality is thought, narrative forms an irreducible dimension of both individual and social identity; it expresses both the objective structures which predetermine the subjective operations of consciousness and the intentionality of subjective consciousness. Narrative structures are ontological in that they are grounded in the 'prenarrative capacity' of life understood as a 'being-demanded-to-be said' inherent to the structure of human action and experience (1991a: 19). Narrative interpretation is central to action in that it is only possible to distinguish it from the biological phenomena of physical movement or psycho-physiological behaviour, through the utilization of the networks of expressions and concepts provided in natural language. Through a synthesis of the heterogeneous elements of experience, narrative plays a key role in the endowment of human practices with meaning; it is constitutive of a 'semantics of action' (1991b: 433).

The narrative interpretation of experience points to the symbolic nature of human action: if human action can be narrated, it is because it is inherently symbolic in nature. The same movement of the arm, for example, can be understood, in different contexts, as a form of greeting, as hailing a taxi, or as casting a vote. Action is only readable because it is symbolic (1991b: 434). Comprehension of human action is not only dependent on familiarity with its symbolic mediation, but also with the temporal structures that evoke narration. Experience is always ascribed a 'virtual narrativity' evident, for example, in psychoanalysis which implies that the story of a life arises from the reconfiguration of untold and repressed stories into 'effective stories which the subject can be responsible for and which he takes as constitutive of his personal identity' (1991b: 435).

Ultimately, narrative structures mediate a tension between stasis and change. Narrative imputes meaning and coherence to the flux of events but can never achieve closure in that it must, to some degree, accommodate the emergence of new possibilities. Ricoeur explores the interplay of stasis and change within identity through the categories of *idem* (sameness) and *ipse* (selfhood). In Ricoeur's view, many thinkers have failed to recognize the constitutive role played by narrative in the construction of personal identity and thereby reduce it to a static, atemporal category of sameness (idem). Idem notions of identity cannot offer a dynamic, temporalized account of the self (ipse) as constancy through and within change. Idem identity implies permanence in time in terms of sameness and similitude and it finds its paradigmatic expression in numerical identity (Ricoeur 1992: 116). The qualitative notion of identification corresponds to this idea of idem identity in the sense that is based on a notion of extreme resemblance, where cognition is recognition (1992: 116). Idem identity is not reducible to corporeal identity, but obviously the acquistion of embodied identity through a process of symbolic identification falls under the sign of idem.

The weakness of the criterion of similitude or physical continuity for an understanding of identity is that it cannot fully account for the question of change in time which may erode resemblance. Ricoeur gives the example of how, with distance in time, resemblance becomes suspicious as a plea for identity in the case of the trials of war criminals (1993: 104–5). There is, then, a notion of permanence or continuity in time that is not reducible to the question of a substratum of similitude or the perpetuation of the same: 'Is there a form of permanence in time which can be connected to the question of "who?" inasmuch as it is irreducible to any question of "what?"? Is there a form of permanence in time that is a reply to the question "Who am I?"?' (1992: 118). This more abstract notion of identity is ipseity or selfhood that necessarily invokes a notion of futurity or change illustrated in the instances of the promise and friendship that imply a constancy of the self through and within change.

Identity is constituted through a fusing and overlapping of the idem and ipse identity. Ipse announces itself as idem in so far as the question of 'who am I?' is overlapped by the question of 'what am I?' For example, selfhood is always understood partially through reference to constant corporeal and psychological criteria such as character and habits (1992: 128). At the same time, these two dimensions of identity are irreducible to each other in so far as they are separated by what Ricoeur calls an 'interval of sense' opened up by the polarity of the two models of permanence in time (1992: 124). It is in narrative that the mediation of these two temporal dimensions of identity is sought. Without recourse to narration, the subject would be condemned to an antinomy. Either the theorist would have to posit, in an idealist fashion, a subject identical to itself through a diversity of different states, or, she adopts a constructivist assertion that the identical subject is nothing more than a 'substantialist illusion whose elimination brings to light a pure manifold of cognitions, emotions and volitions' (1988: 246). The narration of identity creates a meaningful order from the variability and discontinuities of life by grounding the self in the similitude of idem. At the same time, narrative allows the exploration of the potentialities of the self relatively freed from the actualities of idem character evident, for example, in imaginative and philosophical explorations of the themes of freedom and necessity. In extreme cases, the complete detachment of idem from ipse can result in an apophantic apprehension of the self that provokes narrative crisis. For example, memory of traumatic events is often fragmented, tied to bodily experience and overwhelmingly intense. The threat that these overpowering physical memories pose to a stable sense of identity means that trauma survivors are frequently unable to construct narratives to make sense of themselves and their experiences: the sense of self collapses (Brison 1997).

An important implication of Ricoeur's idea of narrative as an irreducible element in the symbolic construction of identity is the extent to which it throws into question the opposition between essentialist and constructivist approaches to identity. The inherent temporality of the concept reformulates this dichotomy between fixity and contingency so that the formation of the subject has the dynamic unity of narrative configuration. This dynamic concept of unity establishes a potentially fruitful convergence with feminist attempts to understand gender identity as durable but not immutable.

Beyond stasis and change

The implications of an understanding of identity in terms of
ipseity for thought on gender may, at first sight, seem rather
obscure. Ricoeur develops the concept primarily in the direction of its ethical ramifications in that the idea of constancy
through change, exemplified in the promise or in friendship,
implies a foundational commitment of the self to other (Ricoeur
1992: 169–202). However, the dialectic of idem–ipse has important ramifications for a social theoretical understanding of
identity in that it yields a conception of the self somewhere
in between the self-reflexive Cartesian ego and the pure contingency of the Nietzschean subject: it mediates between
'the pseudo-alternative of pure change and absolute identity'
(Ricoeur 1991b: 437). The self has unity, but it is the dynamic
unity of narrative which attempts to integrate permanence in
time with its contrary, namely diversity, variability, discontinuity and instability. Most significantly, the idea of narrative as
an irreducible element in the construction of coherent identity
through time throws into question the opposition between
essentialist and anti-essentialist approaches to identity by undoing the attendant dichotomy between fixity and contingency.
Identity is neither completely in flux nor static; it has the
dynamic unity of narrative configuration.

The tendency to think the coherence of the self in the negative terms of an imposed, illusory effect that is the result of
the constructionist critique of the unified subject is underpinned by an attenuated understanding of the contingent or
relational nature of identity. The process through which identity receives its form and substance is derived from the structural understanding of meaning as the product of a series of
differences (Dews 1995: 4–5). An implication of this formal
account of the relational nature of identity is that it often
invokes a rather unqualified notion of contingency where there
are as many possible subject positions as meanings. This is

evident in, for example, Laclau and Mouffe's idea of 'relations
of equivalence', which gives little sense of the embeddedness
of certain types of identity which may prevent their re-
articulation into new discursive formations. In Žižek's terms,
Laclau and Mouffes's work offers a theory of political
subjectivization, but it lacks a concept of the subject who
precedes and constantly thwarts the process of interpellation
(Žižek 1999: 181–2). Such an underdetermined theorization
of the contingency of identity results in a nominalism which
validates the notions of plurality and instability *per se*, manifest, for example, in Douglas Kellner's tendentious claim that
'the overwhelming variety of subject positions, of possibilities
for identity, in an affluent image culture no doubt create highly
unstable identities while constantly providing new openings
to restructure one's identity' (Kellner 1992: 174). A similar
valorization of instability is evident in Bauman's claim that the
problem of postmodern identity is 'primarily how to avoid
fixation and keep the options open' (Bauman 1995: 81).

Feminists have criticized this nominalist understanding of
identity as pure contingency as part of a more wide-ranging
critique of some of the false antitheses that the debate over
essentialism generated. Most feminists now recognize that the
debate during the 1970s was overpolarized and that the term
essentialism has become an 'exegetical cliché' almost devoid of
analytical content (Brennan 1989: 6–9). In an attempt to break
from the dichotomized conceptions of identity as fixed or contingent, feminists have argued that gender is not simply one of
a series of possible subject positions, but a foundational symbolic distinction central to societal reproduction. It is difficult,
if not impossible, to have a socially meaningful existence outside of the norms of gender identity in a way that is not the
case for, say, national or religious identities; as Butler puts it:
'if human existence is always gendered existence, then to stray
outside of established gender is in some sense to put one's very
existence into question' (Butler 1987: 132). Constructionist
accounts of the relational nature of identity often fail to capture the depth and ineluctability of gendered significations in
the construction of identity. Rosi Braidotti's essay on the 'politics of ontological difference' represents an attempt to transcend

the antithesis of constructionist and essentialist conceptions of the subject through a reformulated notion of essentialism as a historical category. Being a woman is neither a biological nor a historical fact; rather it involves the inherence of the two: gender identity is socially determined, but it is not entirely contingent in so far as femininity invariably attaches itself to female bodies. The irreducible inherence of the biological and cultural establishes sexual difference as an ontological phenomenon in that 'being a woman is always already there as the ontological precondition for my existential becoming as a subject' (Braidotti 1989: 102). The claim that gender has ontological foundations leads to the redefinition of essentialism not as a fixed biological or pre-cultural identity but as an historical category which recognises and affirms the totality of definitions that have been made of women: 'Far from being prescriptive in an essentialist-deterministic way, it opens up a field of possible "becoming", providing the foundation for a new alliance among women, a symbolic bond among women *qua* female sexed beings' (Braidotti 1989: 102).

Braidotti's work represents an interesting attempt to configure gender identity beyond the dichotomy of stasis and change unleashed by the essentialist debate and to explain what Catherine MacKinnon calls the 'universal singularity' of women's experience. Yet by according gendered corporeality an ontological status over other structures such as race and class, she finishes by reasserting a problematic originary sexual difference which undermines the historicizing impulse of her work (Moore 1994: 20). Ricoeur's thought provides an interesting contrast because, by insisting on the irreducible temporality of the narrativized self, he goes further than Braidotti in undoing the conflation of ontological arguments with an imputation of a fixed core to identity. A potential objection to Ricoeur's notion of the self is that the attribution of an ontological status to narrative introduces a tacitly transcendental concept of identity (e.g. Anderson 1993). Ipseity, however, is not to be understood as some transcendental essence of self that can withdraw from empirical reality. Rather selfhood is historical *ab initio*; it does not presume a fixed essence beyond the fact of the inherent temporality of human existence.[4] Narrative is an ontological structure in so far as it is the privileged medium through which the temporality of human existence is thought. Narrative might be necessary to grasping the temporal nature of subjectivity, however, it does not impute an unchanging core to the self. It is neither totalizing in that there are always aspects of human existence that escape unification in narrative (Ricoeur 1998: 88). Nor is it the sole means through which temporality is grasped: there are modalities other than narrative through which time is experienced, such as the lyrical aspects of consciousness (1998: 93). Narrative does not exhaust the question of self-constancy. Yet, narrative is ontological or quasi-ontological in that, against Louis Mink for example, Ricoeur does not think that there can be a radical gap between experience and narrative in which the latter is simply violently imposed on the former (Mink 1970). Experience has a pre-narrative structure or nascent narrativity that seems, in many cases, to demand expression: 'our narrative interpretations do not function ex nihilo but follow naturally upon the structure of experience' (Kerby 1991: 42). At the same time, this quasi-narrative structure should not be understood as a realm of experience prior to and fully amenable to expression in language. Nonetheless, although it is neither originary nor totalizing, narrative is necessary to the formation of coherent identity.

The ontological conception of narrative provides a way of thinking of the durability of certain forms of gender identity in terms which are neither normative nor nominalist. It is the temporal structures through which identity is mediated that give gender its durability. Thus an ontologization of sexual difference is avoided. Identity is contingent upon a particular set of social relations; it is not fixed, but neither is it purely arbitrary in that some narratives have deep historical resonance and durability. *Contra* notions of a free-floating contingency, narrative provides a way of conceptualizing how identity has shape and a relative inertness that makes it resistant to change. For Ricoeur, meaning is not just an effect of the relational structure of language but it is also an 'event', that is, the product of a living medium of communication. The plurivocity of discourse is not a function of words in themselves, but an effect of context and the creative nature of intersubjective communication (Ricoeur 1974). The notion of narrative captures this sociocentric idea of meaning as event by suggesting that, whilst it is open to reconfiguration, the mutability of identity is constrained and overdetermined by culturally sanctioned meta-narratives that form the parameters of self-understanding. Narrative is a manner of speaking that imposes a certain number of exclusions and restrictive conditions that the more open concept of discourse – commonly used in post-structural thought – does not necessarily imply. The self may always be in a state of reconfiguration in order to incorporate the flux of experience; however, it is not completely arbitrary or open-ended.

The entrenched nature of narratives of gender can be seen in the confusion and forms of backlash that have occurred as a response to the process of gender restructuring which has been unfolding over the last thirty years. In many respects, narratives expressing traditional gender norms are at odds with the increasing instability and complexity of the concrete practices of men and women. Heterosexual norms – expressed through the narrative of romantic love, marriage, reproduction and fidelity – are belied by the rise in divorce rates, the decline in child-bearing, women's entry into employment and so forth. The recalcitrance of these narratives is indicative of their embeddedness in institutional practices and individual dispositions. The fact that certain narratives remain powerful even though they do not correspond to prevailing circumstances points not only to their historical embeddedness but to their centrality in the maintenance of coherent identity. It is the foundational nature of certain narratives to the expression of coherent identity that is not recognized in much poststructural thought, for example, Lyotard's (1984) declaration of the obsolescence of grand narratives in the era of late modernity.

Although the lives of individuals are shaped within the parameters suggested by culturally sanctioned meta-narratives, individual identity does not simply bear the imprint of these forces. The coherence and durability of patterns of gendered behaviour, say, are not just imposed from without but also emerge from investments made by the individual in certain

narratives. The temporal flux of existence motivates individuals to construct coherent notions of selfhood which may
act as powerful constraints on the ways in which the radical or
unanticipated is incorporated into self-understanding. For
example, Jo VanEvery draws attention to the way in which
women's perceptions of their future roles as wives and mothers
can constrain the development of their working lives (VanEvery
1995: 45). Narratives and the psychological dispositions they
inculcate can become so entrenched that they 'finally become
recipes for structuring experience itself . . . for not only guiding
the life narrative up to the present but directing it into the
future' (Bruner 1987: 31). In other words, the durability of
narratives of gender resides partly in terms of an attachment
on the part of the individual to the sense of stability they
impart – even if it is at the price of their subjection. It is this
form of attachment generated from within which is revealed
by a hermeneutic perspective and is overlooked in the idea
of coherent identity as a discursively imposed fiction which
derives from the negative paradigm of subjectification.

Ricoeur's use of narrative to mediate the opposition of stasis
and change helps to unravel certain other dualisms within
thought on subjectivity, one of them being the dualism of
authentic experience versus ideological distortion. A claim
underlying Riceour's assertion of the ontological status of narrative is, as we have seen, that all social action is inherently
symbolic. All action and experience requires interpretation
and it is in the act of interpretation that narrative acquires
its centrality. The assertion of the symbolic status of action
reframes the relation between ideology and individual practices which is normally conceptualized in terms of distortion
or mystification. It also suggests that there is no sense in which
a hermeneutic understanding of the narrativized self can be
understood as a retreat to an originary subjectivity. The narrative structure of self-identity is neither authentic nor ideological
but an unstable mixture of fact and fabulation. In the next
section, I will show how this problematizes distinctions between ideological and primary narratives made in certain
feminist microsociological work. Like Bourdieu's idea of regulated liberties, it resonates with recent feminist work on the

ambivalent relation between women and dominant conceptions of femininity.

Ideological and primary narratives

An ontological conception of narrative points towards the inherently symbolic nature of all action. Meaning is not inherent to action but is the product of intrepretative strategies amongst which narrative is central. In other words, the concept of agency that emerges neither rests upon an idea of unmediated practice nor does it dismiss action as an illusion of free will. One of the implications of the claim that action is symbolic in nature is that it throws into doubt conventional 'negative' conceptions of ideology which, to some degree, are based on a notion of an illusory distortion of the objective structure of action. If action derives its significance from interpretation, then any distinction between ideological and other narratives on the grounds of a separation between reality and illusion is problematic because all narratives are interpretative in nature. Narrative order is neither false in the sense that it constitutes an illusory coherence imposed upon the heterogeneity of experience; nor does it signify authenticity in that narration always effects a metaphorization of the real.

This understanding of narrative problematizes some of the assumptions of standpoint theory and other types of interpretative feminism which attribute an 'authentic' status to women's social experience. For example, Dorothy Smith's work on the everyday presumes a rupture in social consciousness between women's daily experience – 'primary narratives' – and formal, impersonal modes of interpretation – 'ideological narratives' – that form part of an 'apparatus of ruling' (Smith 1990: 142). Smith explicitly rejects a simple distinction between ideological and primary narratives, arguing that there is always an imbrication of pre-given interpretative schemata within individual self-understanding to the extent that there is no 'one objective account of what actually happened' (1990: 157). Her implicit reliance, however, on a Schutzian notion of a presocial origin to consciousness results in an over-rigid distinction in which primary narratives are seen to adequate more closely than ideological narratives to the original temporal sequence of a given experience: 'Interpretations are, in principle, to be checked against the original experience that the narrative "recapitulates"' (1990: 159). Ideological narratives do not proceed in this fashion in that the formal encoding of experience for a particular end (for example, legal discourse) is highly selective and imposes a 'conceptual agenda' that is not concerned with matching the raw material of the original experience (1990: 160).

Ricoeur's notion of the pre-interpretative or inherently symbolic nature of experience throws into question the idea that there can be any originary, raw material of experience against which the 'deviation' of more abstracted levels of discourse can be checked. The inherent connectivity of narrative meaning, that is, that meaning emerges only by placing events in temporal and spatial relationships with other events, questions the idea that a primary or original experience can be recovered (Somers and Gibson 1994: 59). The construction of any narrative, primary or otherwise, always involves an imaginative process of configuration that results in 'an unstable mixture of fabulation and actual experience' (Ricoeur 1992: 162). In short, all narratives involve a degree of objectification of and distantiation from given events such that 'there is no escape from the politics of representation' (Hall 1996: 473).

If the inherently symbolic nature of experience means that there can be no narrative of authentic experience, on the one side, then it also implies that there can be no pure ideological narrative, on the other. Ideology operating through the medium of narrative clearly has a distortive function evident in the 'simplification, schematization, stereotyping and ritualization' of its forms (Ricoeur 1991a: 182). However, the idea that these distortions are illusory obscures the extent to which ideology can only be effective because it in some way connects to social life: 'unless social life has a symbolic structure, there is no way to understand how . . . reality can become an idea or how real life can produce illusions; these would all be simply mystical and incomprehensible events' (Ricoeur 1986: 8). Ideology then has integrative as well as dominatory effects;

it reinforces social identity, both individual and collective, through a process of 'iconic augmentation' that draws on the pre-interpreted elements of social life and reconfigures them into new symbolic forms. For example, social integration is achieved through the repetition and reinforcement of the mediatory symbolic forms – narratives and chronicles – through which a given community constructs and maintains its origins and identity (Ricoeur 1991a: 196). Specifically, the role of ideology is to conceal any potential tension between the claims of legitimacy made by an authority and the belief in legitimacy on the part of its subjects through the assertion of identity in the face of the antagonistic nature of social experience (Ricoeur 1986: 260–1). Ideology then takes the form of a 'surplus value' in the sense that authority requires an excess of belief in order to legitimate itself: 'the difference between the claim made and the belief offered signifies the surplus value common to all structures of power' (1986: 14). It is in generating this surplus value that the positive and negative aspects of ideology as integration and domination converge. The integrative effect becomes distortive when authority is understood as domination, when open-ended social relationships are frozen into rigid hierarchies, when schematization and rationalization prevail (Ricoeur 1986: 260–6). However, this 'pathological' form of ideology never completely predominates; it is always offset by its underlying integrative function which prevents any antagonism reaching its destructive point and renders ideology an 'open system'.

Like Bourdieu's idea of regulated liberties, the idea of ideology as an 'open system' suggests a way of understanding the relation between women and dominant representations of femininity in terms other than those of dissimulation and misrecognition. The main problem with construing the symbolic construction of gender identity as the imposition of a patriarchal ideology is that the discontinuous nature and effects of representations of femininity are disregarded, producing a coherent, unified feminine subject as a substrate of subordination (Adams 1990: 107). The identification of women with, say, conventional notions of femininity is not a purely negative one of mis-identification but can be understood in terms of a host of other functions suggested, for example, in Holloway's (1984) notion of investment. Ideological images may momentarily stabilize meanings, allowing individuals to identify with or against persons or situations. This is suggested in Winship's work on young women's magazines which, she claims, articulate visual codes of femininity in such a way as to offer readers a more assertive and confident sense of independent femininity (Winship 1985). The narrativizing of marginal experiences, whilst essential to the establishment of submerged female identities, never takes place in isolation from pre-given ideological forms. For a narrative to be meaningful and to acquire some degree of social authority, it must draw to some extent on culturally dominant discourses of truth-telling; this involves a process of autonomization where a given narrative transcends relevance to its initial situation (Ricoeur 1991a: 153–4). The illocutionary force of a narrative cannot reside in a putative privileged relation to true life, but emerges from its partial objectification in symbolic and ideological forms (Gilmore 1994: 23–4). This is not to deny the role of ideological narratives in the maintenance of oppressive social hierarchies, but it is to suggest that the relation between narrative self-understanding and meta-narratives of femininity is more complex and unstable than Smith's distinction between primary and ideological narratives allows.

Imagination and action

Ricoeur's argument that the function of ideology cannot be explained only as distortion draws attention to the negative terms in which the concept is conventionally conceptualized. In his view, ideology is an example of the foundation of society in an irreducible capacity for creativity: the social imaginary. When the implications of this idea are extended to the subject of ideology, then a more creative notion of agency unfolds. Just as Bourdieu develops the idea of a creative substrate to action (*ars inveniendi*) vis-à-vis power and social position, so Ricoeur unfolds some of the ramifications of the same idea for an interpretative understanding of agency. The foundational role that imagination occupies in action counters the exclusionary logic of the negative paradigm of subjectification by suggesting that the relation to the other is not based only on dynamics of disavowal and exclusion.

The significance of the notion of creativity to Ricoeur's thought has been discussed by many commentators, for example, Richard Kearney's work on the idea of the productive imagination (Kearney 1991). However, the implications of the idea of creativity for a theory of agency have been not so widely considered within social theory (Thompson 1981). Ricoeur uses the term creativity to denote the extent to which imagination, as it unfolds in anticipatory consciousness, is constitutive of action to the extent that there is 'no action without imagination' (1994: 126). In the essay 'Imagination in Discourse and Action', Ricoeur extends the exploration of the idea of the productive imagination from a theory of semantic innovation in metaphor to the idea of agency. There are four key respects in which it is impossible to understand action without reference to the anticipatory or projective function of imagination. First, imagination plays a central role in determining a course of action, or the noematic content of a project. It is only by imaginatively trying out different possible courses of action – the overlapping of narrative play with pragmatic play – that an individual is able to take up a particular course of action. Second, it is within the 'luminous clearing' established by the practical imagination that it is possible to differentiate between the various motivations of an action such as desires, ethical, logical or physical constraints: 'The imagination provides the mediating space of a common "fantasy" for things as diverse as the force which pushes as if from behind, the attraction which seduces as if from in front, reasons which justify and establish as if from underneath' (1994: 126). Third, it is in the realm of practical imagination that individuals try out their capacity to do something in the sense of 'I could have done otherwise if I had wanted'. The role of the imagination at these three levels pertains to the phenomenology of individual action. However, illustrating Ricoeur's belief that a critical hermeneutics cannot remain at the level of individual action, imagination is also shown to play a crucial role at a fourth level of the mediation of intersubjective relations. It is only possible to understand a historical field of action through the imposition of categories of common action upon the temporal flux of experience. These common categories of action establish complex relations of 'pairing' between temporal fields; for example, it establishes the relations between contemporaries, predecessors and successors partially through the transmission of tradition. This pairing of diverse temporal fields is achieved through a process of 'analogical apperception' understood as a transcendental principle which, in some sense, establishes the other as another self like myself: 'The imagination is the schematism belonging to the constitution of intersubjectivity in analogical apperception. This schematism functions in the same way as the productive imagination in objective experience, namely, as the genesis of new connections' (1994: 128). In short, imagination is constitutive not just of individual action but also of intersubjective relations and collective forms of action.

Ricoeur's formulation of the central role played by imagination in action suggests forms of relation between self and other that cannot be so readily derived from the negative paradigm of subjectification. The relational dynamic that asserts that identity is established through the exclusion of alterity forecloses an explanation of the subject's capacity to relate to an other in terms other than a negative dynamic of the disavowal of difference. The idea of analogical apperception suggests that the process of subjectification also involves the capacity to establish relatively open and constructive relations with the other. While any form of identity presupposes some exclusion, that does not mean that exclusion becomes the essence of subjectivity. As Fraser puts it: 'Where such exclusions do exist, are they all bad? Are they all equally bad? Can we distinguish legitimate from illegitimate exclusions . . . Is subject-authorization inherently a zero-sum game?' (Fraser 1995: 68; see also Weir 1996: 7). The dynamic of disavowal is not sufficient to explain other, less defensive ways in which subjects relate to the other and how this might be realized in action, for example, in the institution of new forms of social behaviour. A similar point is made by Allison Weir, who argues that, in order to overcome the 'sacrificial logic' that dominates work on identity, it is necessary to develop non-dominatory conceptions of individual identity which emphasize 'the ability of a person to relate to . . . herself and . . . to others in a meaningful way, to act and react self-consciously' (1996: 185). Such a reconceptualization involves the elaboration of clearer distinctions between different elements within subject formation. For example, the capacity for analogical apperception that, in Ricoeur's view, is foundational to the subject's ability to act, implies a potential to relate to the other in an open manner. It denotes the capacity to tolerate alterity and to be able to resolve meaningfully an apparent contradiction. It also runs counter to a dominant strand in constructionist work on identity which tacitly and uncritically valorizes the acceptance of paradox and contradiction as central to non-oppressive subjectivity (e.g. Honig 1996; Young 1990).

Ricoeur's highlighting of the role played by the imagination in the institution of intersubjective relations concurs with various feminist attempts to conceptualize agency in other than rational or instrumental terms. While constructionist accounts of subject formation certainly do not deploy a rational concept of agency, the tendency to neglect the role of intersubjective dynamics in favour of the monological dynamic between subject and symbolic structure leaves it with a similarly diminished understanding of the creative substrate to action. Certain types of relational feminism, for example, highlight the extent to which communicative structures reveal a cooperative or normatively oriented dimension to agency. From a psychoanalytical perspective, Allison Weir claims that the work of Julia Kristeva offers an alternative model of subject formation understood not just as the introjection of the repressive law of the symbolic, but as a capacity for the coherent expression of non-identity. A problem with these formulations is that the relational dynamic between self and other is often tacitly sentimentalized and valorized. For example, it is an established criticism that object relations feminism sentimentalizes and naturalizes the relational dynamic by construing it around a desexualized view of the mother–child dyad (e.g. Flax 1993: 67). Although Habermasian feminists deploy a more sociological account of the intersubjective dynamic, they tend to invoke a domesticated view of otherness or difference in order to maintain the symmetry of the communicative ideal. Similarly, by emphasizing the subject's capacity for the reconciliation and supersession of difference, Weir replicates an error of Habermasian feminists, namely the underestimation of the intractable and destabilizing effects of certain forms of difference for an intersubjective dynamic.

A key difference for Ricoeur is that, although the imagination plays a fundamental role in the institution of analogical or intersubjective relations, the relational dynamic is not tacitly valorized. This is partly achieved by moving beyond an interpersonal understanding of the relational dynamic. The mediation of imaginative connections takes place at the collective level in the social imaginary through, for example, the schemata of ideology and utopia and can, therefore, take the form of hate as much as love, of antagonism as much as consensus. It is at the level of the social imaginary that relations of imaginative transference become distorted and reified, resulting in social inequalities. Furthermore, *contra* Weir, Ricoeur's idea of the narrative structure of identity proposes a more dynamic model which regards the active accommodation of difference as a process rather than an outcome. Narrative self-formation is never complete or fully coherent. In order to draw out a more active conception of agency, it is sufficient to make the weaker case that individuals have the potential to respond in a non-defensive and occasionally creative fashion to complexity and contradiction regardless of whether these differences are effectively reconciled or not.

Identification–disidentification

The tendency in certain feminist thought to valorize the relational dynamic is symptomatic of a broader split in feminist theory in the treatment of non-identity. On the one side, relational feminism denies radical alterity by privileging the subject's ability to reabsorb difference back into the self. On the other side, the idea of non-identity is celebrated in the

importance accorded by constructionist feminism to a politics
of desire based on a refusal of identification with stable subject
positions. This refusal of the category of identity *per se* has
problematic consequences because it often results in a rejection of associated terms such as autonomy and reflexivity
which are central to conceptualizing agency within discourses
on gender. As we have seen in the previous chapter, Bourdieu
challenges the tendency to impute an apodictic radicality to
a politics of desire by an insistence on situating it within the
broader context of the power relations that operate within and
across fields. Ricoeur's work on self-identity questions this
fetishization of the inchoate in a different way by suggesting
that the identical and non-identical are inextricable and in-
trinsic to any process of self-formation. This in turn suggests
renewed grounds for a feminist engagement with the concepts
of autonomy and reflexivity.

Despite acknowledgement of their inseparability, the tendency to disconnect the moments of identity and non-identity
manifests itself in the dualisms of the normal and the excluded, the central and the marginal that tacitly operate in
work on subject formation. For example, on an explicit level,
Judith Butler uses the concept of disidentification derived from
the work of Michel Pêcheux to capture the ambiguities inherent to the process of identification through which subjectivity
is stabilized. Disidentification denotes a relation to dominant
norms which is neither one of recognition and consent (identification) nor refusal and rebellion (counter-identification); it
refers to a form of dislocation arising from the deployment of
the tools and symbols of the dominant by the marginalized, a
'working on the subject form' from within (Hennessy 1993).
In theory, disidentification is characteristic of all modes of
subject formation, yet a tacit separation emerges where identification becomes the mode of recognition of the 'coherent
subject' and disidentification the mode of recognition of the
excluded non-subject. In other words, the moments of identification and distantiation become separated, evident in the
engendering of a further opposition between a politics of identity which cannot 'afford to acknowledge the exclusions upon
which it is dependent' because of its 'dangerous insistence' on

the coherence of the self and a politics of resignification which risks the 'incoherence of identity' through an 'unravelling of the symbolic' (1993: 113–16). The 'false antithesis' between identification and disidentification does not adequately explain the internal inconsistencies within the social construction of gender identity, nor does the idea of disidentification on its own provide sufficient grounds for an understanding of political agency. Albeit inadvertently, Butler seems to assert the inherent subversiveness of the act of symbolic resignification *per se* and endorses a politics of non-identity based on a celebration of the inchoate; as Fraser notes, 'Butler's approach does not give us all we need. Its internal normative resources – reification of performativity is bad, dereification is good – are far too meager for feminist purposes' (Fraser 1995: 162; see also Hill 1987).

The valorization of non-identity is tangentially expressed in a suspicion of what are regarded as the abstract concepts of autonomy and reflexivity. This refusal of abstraction originates with the feminist critique of patriarchal thought and the implicitly masculinist nature of its supposedly objective categories. Abstraction, or the perspective of the general other, is regarded as based on a denial of the connection to the other and on a disavowal and derogation of the embodied condition in general. For Butler, the capacity for abstraction is regarded as problematic because it is based on a separation of the subject from its cultural predicates (Butler 1990: 143–4; Weir 1995: 267). Like the dismissal of the category of identity, the rejection of any form of abstract thought arises from the negative conception of subject formation as always-already exclusionary. It may be necessary, however, to question the validity of such a blanket rejection because of the theoretical and political impasse in which it leaves feminist thought in terms of conceptualizing agency. As Diana Fuss puts it, 'identification is only one philosophical approach to the problem of alterity' (Fuss 1995: 9). If the ability to act implies some form of transcendence from immediate material circumstances, then an unequivocal insistence on the embeddedness of the subject undermines ways in which to think of agency with respect to transformations in gender norms.

By sketching out the necessary intertwinement of the moments of identification and distantiation, Ricoeur shows how the capacity for autonomous thought or action is a potential immanent to the process of subject formation, rather than being based on a denial of the embedded and embodied condition. This is suggested by disaggregating the mimetic process that underlies the narrative construction of the self into three levels. The stages of prefiguration, configuration and refiguration propose a more active process of self-interpretation predicated on a simultaneity rather than diremption of the moments of identification and disidentification.[5] The implications of the idea of the centrality of distantiation to self-understanding for a theory of agency are most explicit, however, in Ricoeur's mediation of the debate between Habermas and Gadamer over explanation (erklären) and understanding (verstehen).

From Gadamer's hermeneutic perspective, the 'alienating distantiation' or separation that permits the establishment of an objectifying attitude in the human sciences must be refuted because all human understanding is historically situated and, therefore, finite. The idea of complete objectivity is illusory; there can be no transcendent perspective from which an exhaustive critique of prejudice or ideology is possible. Thus the task of hermeneutics is to uncover the historical and traditional grounds upon which knowledge is based. Hermeneutic analysis emphasizes the moment of 'belonging', of participation in historical reality which is conventionally constructed as an object of knowledge but, in fact, constitutes the ontological grounds of all forms of knowledge. The notion of distantiation that underlies the objectifying perspective is an illusion that destroys the necessarily historical and finite nature of knowledge. The critical moment can only be developed as an instant subordinated to the consciousness of finitude and of dependence upon the figures of pre-understanding which always precede and envelop it. As Ricoeur puts it: 'Historical knowledge cannot free itself from the historical condition. It follows that the project of a science free from prejudices is impossible . . . Man's links to the past precedes and envelops the purely objective treatment of historical facts' (Ricoeur 1981: 76).

Against the hermeneutic insistence on the situated nature of knowledge, Habermas defends the possibility of an exhaustive critique of the prejudice – that is, the critique of ideology – that distorts human thought. In his view, the critique of ideology, which underpins the emancipatory impulse of the critical social sciences, must proceed not from the assumed primacy of tradition over judgement, but from the regulative ideal of unlimited and unconstrained communication. The mistake of the hermeneutic perspective is that it ontologizes the historical preconditions of knowledge as the ready-made and unsurpassable horizon of being such that the force of tradition and authority forbid critical distantiation. For Habermas, it is the task of the critical social sciences to identify 'ideologically frozen relations of dependence' in order to overcome them. The critical approach is governed by an interest in emancipation or a moment of self-reflection which leads to autonomy. It is the interest in autonomy 'which shows the dependence of the theoretical subject on empirical conditions stemming from institutional constraints and which orients the recognition of these forms of constraint towards emancipation' (Ricoeur 1981: 83). Critique is forward rather than backward looking; it cannot ground itself on an *a priori* consensus for what is prior is distorted and broken communication. Critique is anticipatory in that it is grounded in the regulative ideal of an unlimited and unconstrained communication. Thus, for Habermas, distantiation is a necessary moment of critique, close to a Kantian imperative.

The positions of both Habermas and Gadamer raise difficulties that parallel problems with the feminist critique of abstract concepts such as autonomy through the idea of embeddedness. The hermeneutic suspicion of distantiation discourages any critical moment in thought, while the Habermasian ideal of undistorted communication is conceptualized in such an abstract and formal manner that it seems to forget that all knowledge is, to some degree, historically determined and partial. As Ricoeur points out, the utopian moment of undistorted communication can only be derived from a creative reinterpretation of our preceding cultural heritage: 'if we had no experience of communication, however restricted or mutilated it was, how could we wish it to prevail for all men and at all institutional levels of the social nexus?' (Ricoeur 1981: 97). In Ricoeur's view, the apparent impasse between the acknowledgment of the finite nature of knowledge and the critique of ideology can be overcome if the relation between the moments of belonging and distantiation is formulated in a dialectical rather than a dichotomous fashion. The moment of distantiation characteristically belongs to interpretation and this mediatory notion is explored through the problematic of the text, which is regarded as the paradigm of distantiation in communication.

Distantiation in the text, which is not reducible to writing, takes four forms. First, distantiation occurs in the dialectic of event and meaning that is constitutive of discourse. The definition of discourse as event directs attention to language as the actualization of linguistic competence and therefore to the subject who speaks and to whom it is directed and to its referential function (Ricoeur 1974). However, discourse does not only have the character of an event, for the actual fleeting moment of the 'saying' is necesssarily surpassed in the meaning that endures, the said. Thus the first moment of distantiation is the distantiation of the 'saying in the said' (Ricoeur 1981: 134). The fixation of meaning in writing and all comparable phenomena leads to the autonomy of the text in three further respects: with regard to the intention of the author; with regard to the cultural situation and the sociological conditions of production of the text; and finally with regard to the original addressee. The ability of the text to transcend its original psycho-sociological conditions of production creates a potentially limitless audience and a potentially unlimited series of readings in so far as the autonomization of the text displaces any notion of authorial intentionality. It follows from this that the autonomy of the text that proceeds from the objectification of discourse (of the saying in the said) is constitutive of interpretation rather than, *pace* Gadamer, opposed to it. The freeing of the text from its conditions of reproduction or its ostensive function displaces interpretations of the text in terms of the intentions of the author or responses of the reader. The displacement of intentional readings opens the way to understanding interpretation through the intersection of the projected world of the text with the world of the reader. Here, interpretation revolves not only around understanding the direct matter of a text (first-order reference), but also around the subject's ability to engage with the alternative vision of the world that the text projects 'in front of itself' (second-order reference): 'What must be interpreted is a *proposed world* which I could inhabit and wherein I could project one of my ownmost possibilities. That is what I call the world of the text, the world proper to *this* unique text' (1981: 142). The interpretation of the proposed world that stands in front of the text has implications for the subjectivity of the reader who, in order to understand the text, must not project the self on to the text but must rather relinquish it. The reader must 'unrealize' the self in order to appropriate the text: 'As reader, I find myself only by losing myself. Reading introduces me into the imaginative variations of the *ego*' (1981: 144). This disappropriation of the self is not only the condition of possibility of understanding, but also shows how understanding involves more than a simple act of identification, but also always involves a moment of distantiation which forms the potential for critique and autonomous action (1981: 94–5).

From the theory of textual distantiation, Ricoeur derives an analogous explanation of 'meaningful social action'. Just as the necessary and durable inscription of discourse in the text represents the distantiation of the saying in the said, so meaningful action undergoes a similar process of objectification. In the same way as a text is detached from its author, an action may be detached from its agent and develop consequences of its own. The autonomization of human action constitutes the social dimension of action in so far as it has effects that escape the intentionality of the actor. Through the sedimentation of human action in social time, 'human deeds become "institutions", in the sense that their meaning no longer coincides with the logical intentions of the actors' (Ricoeur 1981: 207). Like the freeing of the text from its ostensive reference, the significance of a meaningful action goes beyond its relevance to a particular situation. It succeeds in transcending the social conditions of its production and may be re-enacted in new social contexts. This transcendence also means that action may address itself to an indefinite range of possible readers and, therefore, to an indefinite range of potential readings: 'human action is an open work, the meaning of which is "in suspense". It is because it "opens up" new references and receives fresh relevance from them, that human deeds are also waiting for fresh interpretations which decide their meaning' (Ricoeur 1981: 208).

Ricoeur's idea of distantiation complicates the diremption of identification–disidentification, immanence and transcendence, by showing that self-formation is always predicated on a moment of disappropriation. In other words, the tension between the moments of distantiation and identification that underlies the assertion of the self may be generative of the capacity for critique. In this way the tendency in the negative paradigm to accord a critical privilege to marginal positions based only on the moment of disidentification is questioned. This is not to deny what Bourdieu calls the lucidity of the excluded but it is to problematize the rather uncritical privileging of the marginal as resistance that often dominates constructionist work on subject formation. The isolation of the moment of identification from that of distantiation upon which this celebration of marginality is based creates problems in Foucault's work which, through the conflation of the terms normative and normalization, loses any sense of the active effort of appropriation that underlies the reproduction of even the most seemingly stable of social norms. Conformity to norms cannot simply be inferred from the existence of norms themselves; it may often be the case that the actor had to devise a new and unfamiliar path of action. It is this capacity for independent and even unexpected action inherent to the most mundane and normatively oriented behaviour that Ricoeur invokes with his notion of the inevitable grounding of the moment of mimetic identification in distantiation. Even when it is not realized in consciousness, the moment of distantiation is inherent to the process through which individuals invest in hegemonic meanings, rendering it constitutively unstable. In this way, Ricoeur's idea of narrative self-interpretation undoes the diremption of identification from disidentification which tacitly prevails in theories of 'excentric' subject formation.

Temporal discontinuity

One way of understanding how the intertwinement of the
identical and the non-identical manifests itself within self-
formation is through the idea of temporal discontinuity which
underpins Ricoeur's account of the construction of narrative
identity. The discursive determinism of the negative paradigm
tends to reduce the question of subjectivity to the idea of idem
or corporeal identity. The temporality expressed in the idea of
ipseity serves as a reminder that subjectivity is caught up with,
but not reducible to, corporeal being (idem). As Simone de
Beauvoir puts it, the body of woman is one of the 'essential
elements' in her situation in the world, but that body is 'not
enough to define her as a woman' (1972: 69). The analogous
reduction of gendered subjectivity to issues of sexuality echoes
the poststructuralist tendency to conflate 'personality structure
and the self' (Joas 1998: 11). Gender is an 'internally complex
structure, where a number of different logics are superimposed
. . . accordingly masculinity, like femininity, is always liable to
internal contradiction and historical disruption' (Connell 1995:
73). Embodied gender norms form a fundamental substrate to
women's social experience, but they are not experienced in a
straightforward or direct fashion. Rather they are mediated
through other social practices and categories (Riley 1988:
1–17). It is this process of mediation that results in the
non-adequation of the gendered self to a corporeal identity and
permits the possibility of autonomous action (Willis 1988: 118).
The notion of ipseity draws attention to this disjunction and to
the phenomenon, noted by Denise Riley, of the intermittent
nature of gendered self-consciousness. Riley's claim is sup-
ported, for example, by Lucy Bailey's research on pregnant
women which suggests that an awareness of their embodied
condition does not dominate their consciousness but is frequently displaced and overlaid by other conceptions of the
self, such as professional identities (Bailey 1999: 155).

One way of construing this movement in and out of gender
is through the idea of the temporal mediation of identity (Riley
1988: 96–7). In short, a hermeneutic understanding of narrative

self-identity provides a way of mapping the ebb and flow of the experience of sexual identity as it is mediated through other social roles and practices. The 'inadequation of narrative and the multiform unity of time' also suggests that gender identity comprises a multiplicity of time forms which are managed to greater or lesser degrees in the everyday lives of men or women (1988: 259). Barbara Adam has argued, for example, that a notion of temporal complexity and discontinuity is central to an understanding of the intricacies of living in a post-traditional order where men and women operate 'in a complexity of times which, in turn, need to be synchronized with the time of significant others and the society within which those employees live and work' (Adam 1995: 104). In feminist work on time, this complexity is often reduced to a dualism where feminine experience tends to be located on the level of everyday temporality understood as cyclical, reproductive and expressive and which falls in the shadow of a masculine temporality understood as progressive, standardized and instrumental (Ermarth 1989). However, such dualist notions of time do not capture adequately the variable effects of detraditionalization and globalization upon women's lives.

Ricoeur's conception of narrative identity as a relatively unstable configuration arising from the incompatibility of the different temporal strands of experience provides a way of mapping this temporal discontinuity with regard to identity formation. This is illustrated, for example, in Karen Davies's work on women's temporal consciousness of the experience of short- and long-term unemployment. Davies uses the notion of 'composite' identity to typify the experience of having to negotiate the divergent temporalities of everyday life (Davies 1990: 26). Contrary to assumptions that women tend to regard paid work as secondary to their roles in the home, or that their other daily activities are discrete and can be clearly ranked in importance, Davies found a more fluid situation where activities could not be hierarchized and that relations between them were in a state of flux. In terms of temporal consciousness, what emerged was a complicated picture of the interweaving of different temporally structured activities: 'the interweaving of cyclical and linear time . . . the clashing of clock and process time (forfeiting care of and time with one's child because of the necessity to work), the fact that there is never any time-out for women' (Davies 1990: 230–1). The dualism of an embodied, feminine temporality versus an instrumental masculine one is also problematized by Bailey's research, which shows that middle-class mothers often deploy segmented, rationalized approaches in organizing their maternal activities while regarding work as a more open and fluid time for the self (Bailey 1999).

The idea of a temporal discontinuity at the heart of narrative identity also yields a more ambiguous view of the detraditionalization of gender relations than that which can be derived from the simplified division between conventional and post-conventional orders that is often deployed (Thompson 1996; Adam 1996). The idea of temporal complexity suggests that change within gender relations is uneven and non-synchronous, arising from the increasingly dysfunctional effects of the dominant economy of clock time for both women and men. Ulrich Beck's (1992) work on the pluralization of life narratives implies a similar notion of the non-synchronicity of change in gender relations. The detraditionalizing forces at work on the social realm – increased life expectancy, contraceptive control, extension of higher education, increased fragility of marriage – are breaking down fixed gender narratives and exposing women in particular to the individualized biographies of the market subject. At the same time as the narratives of traditional gender biographies and the market subject are pulling apart, there is an increasing trend to the simultaneous differentiation and institutional standardization of biographies. The effect on the lives of men and women of having to negotiate this multiplication of narratives is ambiguous. The heightened reflexivity that this process of pluralization may provoke is potentially emancipatory in that it can lead to the renegotiation of gender relations on more egalitarian terms (Giddens 1992). The non-synchronicity of these narrative strands may manifest itself, however, in the increasing difficulty that individuals experience in coordinating the different temporal dimensions of their life: 'when the multiple [temporal] components come adrift, the price to pay . . . can range from illness and accidents, to divorce, strikes and socio-financial hardship' (Adam 1995: 104).

In sum, the idea of narrative identity signals the complex nature of social time which revolves around multiple levels of temporality – tempo, timing, the relation to past, present and future – that are simultaneously lived but not reconcilable. By drawing attention to the irreconcilable levels of temporal experience, narrative provides a model for explaining, from a hermeneutic perspective, the impact that the breakdown of traditional gender relations may have upon the self. If the temporality of experience is not exclusively linear, additive or iterative, then change is experienced not as rupture or smooth progression but in an uneven and negotiated way suggested in Beck's notion of 'biographies in transition' where the way in which one lives becomes the biographical solution of systemic contradictions (Beck 1992: 137). It is the extent to which these multiple temporalities are configured into a coherent pattern that is also suggestive of a more substantive account of agency. The ideas of configuration and refiguration that underlie the narrative construction of identity outline dynamic and interpretative dimensions to agency. Narrative is the mode through which individuals attempt to integrate the non-synchronous and often conflictual elements of their lives and experiences.

Narrative and power

While Ricoeur's idea of narrative identity provides an interpretative perspective on the active role played by the subject in the process of self-formation, the political implications of such an idea cannot be examined without being placed in the context of power relations. This is a weakness of Ricoeur's thought, which, despite its suggestive nature, tends to disregard a close analysis of the ideological and institutional context in which narrative forms operate (Thompson 1981: 127–8). This does not mean that an analysis of power relations could not be incorporated into his thought; indeed, Ricoeur's work on ideology and action clearly touches on such areas. His idea, for example, of the distantiation of action, that agency cannot be reduced to the intentionality of actors but becomes exteriorized and sedimented within social time, clearly raises issues of power such as the relation between individuals and institutions. However, Ricoeur's treatment of the cluster of power relations pertaining to the agency–structure relation is underdeveloped and equivocal in that it often rests on rather tenuous arguments by analogy with the idea of text (Thompson 1981: 126–30).

The feminist concern with understanding how gender differences are transformed into inequalities addresses the connection between narrative and power more explicitly and, in this respect, serves to counterbalance the emphasis on text as a model for action in Ricoeur's work. Culturally sanctioned narratives are central to the imposition of hegemonic identities and the emergence of new or contestatory forms inevitably highlights the relations of power that underlie the production of narrative discourse: 'The channels by which new forms of solidarities are fuelled rely on the capacity of narratives to disclose previously unseen marginalization, exclusion and prejudice' (Lara 1998: 8). In her work on feminist narratives and the public sphere, Maria Pia Lara relies extensively on Ricoeur's notion of narrative while drawing attention to the poverty of his conception of the political realm. The ideas of reflexivity and the relation with the other that are central to the concept of narrative identity lack a critical edge because they fail to thematize the mediating role played by the public sphere in the construction of these relations. The force of Ricoeur's dialogical model of narrative identity is undercut by its resolution into an ethics of recognition based on an individualist model of friendship. In Lara's view, the explicit feminist concern with power exposes more fully how the emergence, contestation and coexistence of narratives is inextricably tied to cultural struggle and relations of illocutionary force. This, in turn, highlights the necessity for a strong public sphere in which conflict between competing narratives may be regulated and respect for the other promoted: 'The normative content of friendship must be firmly grounded in the field of

justice, a fact that is not well thought out in Ricoeur's Aristo-
telian approach' (Lara 1998: 143).

Lara is right to criticize Ricoeur's underdeveloped notion of
the political, yet, at the same time, her discussion of feminist narratives is hampered by a problematic definition of emancipatory
narratives as integrative rather than exclusionary (1998: 5).
Ultimately, this derives from her reworking of Habermas's rather
tendentious privileging of the illocutionary dimensions of speech
acts. Further, Lara's claim that 'women's narratives have an
emancipatory content whatever their particular viewpoints' presumes a rather naive view of the primacy of sexual over other
social divisions, of the coherence of women's experience and of
narration of that experience as inherently integrative and
liberatory (1998: 3). Ricoeur's work on narrative throws into
question any such clear separation of the integrative from the
exclusionary, reminding us that the ideological and utopian are
inextricably interwoven in the stabilization of subjectivity.
In conclusion, there is a fruitful area of convergence between
feminist work on narrative and Ricoeur's ontological conception.
Against Ricoeur, the conditions of production and dissemination
of narrative and the way in which these are connected to the
maintenance of hierarchical gender relations need to be thematized more explicitly in the manner suggested by Bourdieu's
work on the field. However, Ricoeur's understanding of narrative as the fundamental medium through which the temporality
of human experience is thought goes some way to overcoming
certain dichotomous oppositions – stasis (idealism) versus change
(nominalism) and authenticity versus the ideological – in which
negative formulations of subjectivity often become enmeshed.

Conclusion

The idea of a narrative structure to identity supplements the
poststructural dispersion of the subject with an account of the
formation of a more coherent sense of self. Narrative coherence does not emerge from an unchanging core within the self,
but rather emerges from the attempt, on the part of individuals

and societies, to make sense of the temporality of existence. This gives depth to the rather one-dimensional way in which the idea of the contingency of identity has been thematized in poststructural thought. It is the lack of temporal depth in many social constructionist accounts of identity that leaves them unable to mediate the relation between fixity versus change which is one of the oppositions generated by the debate on essentialism. The idea of temporal complexity at the heart of narrative identity offers a way of conceptualizing the mediated nature of gender identity and the uneven and non-synchronous nature of change within gender relations. It also provides a way of explaining the inseparability of the identical and non-identical in subject formation. The dynamic between these two moments is generative of reflexivity: the underlying moment of distantiation that is necessary to the process of self-formation entails the potential for critique. This problematizes simplified distinctions between the central and the marginal which operate in certain theories of gender identity.

4

PSYCHE AND SOCIETY: CASTORIADIS AND THE CREATIVITY OF ACTION

Introduction

This chapter considers the extent to which a psychoanalytic account of subject formation can be integrated into a socially determinate idea of agency. Usually, constructionist and psychoanalytic descriptions of subjectification and agency are seen as mutually exclusive. From a constructionist perspective, the psychoanalytic explanation of subjectivity through archetypal categories forecloses a historically specific account of agency. From a psychoanalytic point of view, the constructionist use of categories such as normalization and internalization are regarded as functionalist in so far as they efface the instabilities within subject formation. Despite its seeming intractability, there is a growing recognition in work on identity that this opposition between theories of psyche and subject needs to be overcome. An understanding of the psychic dimensions of subjectivity is indispensable to a nuanced account of the way in which gender identities operate. It sheds light on both the intensity of investments in norms of masculinity and femininity and the difficulties men and women may have in sustaining those identifications. In short, it adds depth to an account of agency and guards against voluntarism by showing how action may be subverted or intensified by unconscious motivations.

While constructionist concepts of subjectification require greater differentiation in terms of an understanding of different

levels of consciousness and motivation, the problem of the
ahistorical nature of psychoanaytical theory remains. I argue
that recent attempts to incorporate a sense of historical
specificity into an account of the psychic formation of the
subject are hindered by the extent to which they remain within
the negative paradigm of Lacanian theory. Two central difficulties with Lacan's theory are the claim that subjectivity is
constituted around a lack and the formal nature of his conception of the symbolic realm. These result in an overdeterminist
paradigm which precludes a substantive idea of agency. I argue
that the work of the psychoanalytic theorist Cornelius
Castoriadis on the radical and social imaginaries presents an
explicitly historical understanding of the interface between the
psyche and the social which has interesting implications for a
social theoretical account of gender identity.

The fundamental insight of Castoriadis's work is that identity is formed not around a lack, *pace* Lacan, but around an
originary capacity for figuration – the radical imaginary. The
idea of an originary capacity for figuration provides an ontological account of the agent's capacity for creative and autonomous behaviour. It also counters the tendency of the negative
paradigm towards symbolic determinism by suggesting that
the relation between the psyche and the social be understood
as one of mutual inherence or interdependence. Moreover, the
linguistic notion of the symbolic is replaced with the broader
category of the social imaginary which is characterized as the
realm where meaning is both imposed, but also created. This
dynamic of the instituting–instituted is generative of agency
and goes some way to overcoming the seemingly inexorable
negativity that Lacan's model accords to the instauration of
feminine identity. The formulation of the relation between
psyche and society as inherence also reframes the idea of
autonomy as an active–passive relation with the other rather
than as a form of self-containment. In a way that echoes
Ricoeur's work on reflexivity, Castoriadis's reconfiguration of
the concept of autonomy counters certain feminist arguments
that such concepts should be rejected because they express a
form of masculinist abstraction. Rather the idea of autonomy
is central to a reformulated understanding of agency in the

context of the changing relations of power thrown up by the restructuring of gender relations in late-capitalist societies.

Subject and psyche

The opposition between psychoanalysis and social constructionism is one of the central faultlines within thought on subject formation and agency. The differences between the two accounts of subjectification are well rehearsed and, like other theoretical problems in thought on identity, have been unhelpfully polarized by the debate on essentialism. From a constructionist perspective, the weakness of psychoanalysis is that the centrality it accords archetypal dynamics in the process of subject formation forecloses an adequate understanding of the social and cultural variability of agency. This critique of the ahistorical nature of psychoanalysis has its roots partly in the huge influence that Foucault's work has upon constructionist theories of the subject. It is well known that Foucault emphatically rejected psychoanalysis on the grounds that the concept of repression implies a hidden 'truth' or essence to identity which ultimately naturalizes and legitimates normative accounts of subjectivity (Foucault 1978: 129–30). The introspective disposition that the search to understand the psychodynamics of the sequestered self provokes is an exemplary expression of the disciplinary strategy of the 'confessional' which operates through a process of normalization. The urge to confess and divulge one's inner truth eventually becomes so deeply inculcated within individuals that it renders them self-policing subjects (Foucault 1978: 60). Ultimately, this preoccupation with the self reifies identity, obscuring both its arbitrariness and the ways in which it may be subverted and changed.

From a psychoanalytic point of view, the range of concepts such as internalization and normalization which constructionist thought deploys have functionalist overtones and efface the instabilities and complexities inherent to the process of subject formation. Psychoanalytic commentators argue that Foucault simplifies the Freudian notion of repression by detaching it from the category of the unconscious which, far from suggesting a

fixity to identity, indicates its impossibility, through the ideas
of resistance and slippage (Rose 1986). For example, constructionist explanations of the formation of gendered subjectivity
in terms of the sex–gender distinction do not address adequately
the paradoxes internal to subjectification. The distinction does
not explain the deep-rooted and often unconscious attachments to conventional and arguably oppressive notions of
masculinity and femininity held by men and women. Nor do
the ideas of acculturation and normalization, which the sex–
gender couplet presumes, permit sufficient consideration of
the extent to which men and women may experience difficulties
in assuming the normative positions of masculinity and femininity. The psychoanalytical theory of the structuring of desire
around Oedipus provides a compelling explanation of unconscious attachments to masculine and feminine subject positions: why it is that, on a certain level, men and women should
willingly comply with their subjection. In this regard, it provides a more forceful developmental account of the cohesion
or constancy of the self which is often lacking in constructionist
explanations: 'it [psychoanalysis] provides an account of the
continuity of the subject, of the past implicated in the present
and a view of development which is in direct contrast to . . .
oversimplified biological or social determinisms' (Henriques
et al. 1984: 205). The constructionist assertion of the contingency of identity often fails to examine discontinuities between levels of psychic experience and socially available subject
positions. In a critique of the work of Jacques Donzelot, for
example, Parveen Adams has criticized the implied voluntarism
that underlies the idea of normalization. On the one hand, for
the process of normalization to be efficacious, it is assumed
that individuals are not free to choose to accept whatever
normative images are presented to them. However, on the
other hand, the idea of resistance implies that they are able to
stand outside these same norms in order to reject them. This,
however, undercuts the argument about the efficacy of norms
resulting in an aporetic understanding where they are both
insidiously inculcated and freely adopted (Adams 1982). The
complex dynamics of psychic investment are simplified by being
reduced to the dichotomy of rejecting or mirroring prevailing

social norms. Furthermore, changes within the socio-cultural realm may exacerbate discontinuity and lag in that individuals will unconsciously cling to entrenched and residual patterns of behaviour. The psychoanalytical conception of the unconscious, as that which cannot be accommodated within the symbolic realm, provides a powerful account of the impossibility of identity or how the assumption of masculine and feminine positions is neither straightforward nor an ever fully realized process. As Butler puts it: 'the psyche, which includes the unconscious, is very different from the subject: the psyche is precisely what exceeds the imprisoning effects of the discursive demand to inhabit a coherent identity, to become a coherent subject' (1997b: 86).

One of the underlying issues at stake in the opposition between the psychoanalytic and constructionist understanding of the formation of subjectivity is the status that is accorded to the pre-reflexive foundations of agency. In other terms, there is a discrepancy between two different concepts of reflexivity; on the one side, constructionism conceptualizes reflexivity, in the philosophical sense, of a negative or critical mode of self-relation and, on the other side, reflexivity is understood, in the psychoanalytical sense, as a primordial repression where subjugation is internalized and eroticized – the 'regulation of desire' becomes the 'desire for regulation' (Žižek 1999: 290). Although constructionism recognizes the importance of theorizing the pre-reflexive foundations of agency – for example, through ideas of the cultural inscription of the body – the idea of agency often assumes a transcendence of that moment, in the dynamic where reflexive consciousness passes through the other in order to return to itself. In Foucault, as we have seen, the two moments remain theoretically unconnected, producing a vacillation in his work between determinism and voluntarism. Either, the pre-reflexive grounds of subjectivity are accorded so much priority that any notion of agency is stifled in the reduction of indivduals to docile bodies; or, in the idea of an aesthetics of existence, the body is accorded such a degree of plasticity that it forms an unproblematic and pliant backdrop to self-formation. In Bourdieu and Ricoeur, the relation between the pre-reflexive and reflexive aspects of

subjectivity is formulated more dialogically through a thematization of the temporality of the process of subjectification. But
both thinkers produce accounts of agency which underplay
some of the more troubling and destabilizing effects that
irrational and unconscious motivations may have upon an
individual's behaviour. This foreclosure is evident, for example,
in Bourdieu's understanding of an actor's investment within a
field of action which, to a degree, is assimilable to the more
rational concept of interest. In Ricoeur, this tendency is
evident to the extent that the moment of integrity in the narrative construction of the self is necessarily prioritized over
moments of conflict and contradiction in order for the idea
of ipseity to be invested with an ethical force. In sum, the
flattening out of different levels of motivation and consciousness that is often the effect of constructionist thought offers a
simplified explanation of the profound bonds – or what Butler
calls 'passionate attachments' – which tie individuals to irrational or oppressive forms of behaviour and which are essential
to understanding certain dimensions of gendered subjectivity.

The psychic in the social

In attempting to integrate an idea of agency into work on the
formation of gendered subjectivity, many feminists have begun
to break down the obfuscatory oppositions between so-called
ahistorical concepts of the psyche, on the one hand, and functionalist concepts of the subject, on the other. From within
psychoanalysis, feminists have claimed that, far from foreclos-
ing a historically sensitive account of agency, the Lacanian
stress on the impossibility of identity permits an understanding
of variation and change within gendered behaviour. These arguments are well known and only briefly need restating. Rather
than essentializing sexual identity, Lacan's understanding of
the coherence of the subject as an illusion, emanating from the
fundamental lack around which it is constituted, guarantees a
lack of fixity in identity; it reveals that 'there is no stability of
sexual identity, no position for women (or for men) which is
ever simply achieved ... "failure" is something endlessly repeated

and relived moment by moment throughout our individual histories' (Rose 1986: 90–1). Against claims of the pre-given, biological nature of sexual difference, Lacan claims that the psyche is not intrinsically male or female. Sexual identity is constituted through Oedipus and the castration complex which are situated within the phallocentric order of language. By taking up a place in relation to the phallus, Lacan defines the formation of sexual identity as a symbolic, and not a natural, biological phenomenon.[1] The assumption of masculine or feminine identity is not necessarily determined by anatomical distinctions; a biological male may assume a feminine position and vice versa. It is the bar to the feminine within a phallocentric definition of sexual difference which constitutes the grounds of culture and which provides an important non-biologically reductionist account of gender identity.[2] The reconceptualization of Oedipus as a linguistic matrix implies that masculinity and femininity are extremes along an unstable continuum of subject positions which it is possible for men and women to occupy (e.g. Cornell and Thurschwell 1987).

It is precisely the anti-essentialist implications of this linguistic model that, according to certain feminists, permit the introduction of a greater notion of historicity into the psychoanalytic explanation of subject formation. For Drucilla Cornell (1993), for example, the power of Lacan's model is that it does not rest on an idealization of the phallus, but always returns to the problem of Woman as lack, as the repressed truth of man. In doing this, Lacanian psychoanalysis implicitly raises the question of the resymbolization of the maternal function and of the feminine within sexual difference. This process of resymbolization is possible not only because of the symbolic, rather than biological, grounds of identity formation, but also because symbolic constructions of femininity are not conflated with the actual lives of women. The maintenance of this distinction between the social and the symbolic is important if feminist theory is to reconstruct a feminine imaginary which escapes from existing patriarchal definitions of womanhood: 'The impossibility of a simply empirical description of our sexual difference means there is no truth to who we are as women' (Cornell 1995: 86).

Deploying the Derridean notion of iterability, Cornell argues that the notion of the feminine as the limit of meaning within the symbolic should be understood not as an absolute bar, but rather as a metaphor of the excess inherent in all identification: 'The figure as the representation of what cannot be represented expresses both the disruptive power of what remains uncanny and, as a condensation into a figure, the taming of the uncanny. The condensation of the figure points beyond to the metonymy of the signifier Woman which has no fixed signified' (1995: 93). The historicity and, therefore, inherent instability of identity prevents its full institution and points to the ethical possibilities of reworking identity. This dialogical notion of temporality, of a past which cannot be fully recollected ('secondness') and which yields a notion of futurity undetermined by the already actualized past ('thirdness'), is inherent in the Lacanian notion of the 'future anterior' and is central to Cornell's definition of ethical feminism. Ethical feminism is based around a re-exploration of the past in terms of the re-collective imagination which revalues and extends our notion of the meaning of the category of woman. It is also predicated upon an exploration of the 'should be' within representations of the feminine, as a refusal of closure and as an openness to rethinking and justifying our *sittlich* commitments (1993: 36–57).

Despite Cornell's claim that Lacan's idea of the impossibility of identity implicitly permits a radical historical or genealogical understanding of the category of femininity, the idea of the future anterior remains a rather abstract possibility which does not lend itself to a thoroughgoing socio-historical understanding of change. As in Butler's work, a more determinate concept of agency is substituted with a structural potentiality. The social specificity is undercut further by Cornell's tendency to presume the monolithic phallocentrism of the symbolic realm resulting in an understanding of femininity in terms of exclusion which undervalues the actualities of women's concrete existence. Her formulation of the instability of the category of femininity is, in Nancy Fraser's words, 'an abstract promise' that the symbolic order could be otherwise which does little to explain the cultural shifts and conflicts that underlie change within gender norms. Further, it privileges 'the Great Refusal' over existing struggles and 'in its abstract, indeterminate form, Cornell's call to resymbolize "the feminine within sexual difference" entrenches a conceptually and politically dubious gender binarism' (Fraser 1995: 166).

Teresa Brennan approaches the question of the historicity of psychic formations in terms of understanding the intertwinement of the social and the psychic, rather than from the perspective of the indeterminacy of the symbolic. Psychical structures do not exist in isolation and the force with which they manifest themselves at any given time is determined by the socio-historical context (Brennan 1990). In this way, a theoretical space is created for explaining cultural variation and agency. The idea of torsion inherent in the image of the Möbius strip is used to thematize a relation of non-exhaustive mutual determination to explain the relation between psyche and society.[3] The content of the psyche is not simply a repository for social determinations; nor, however, do psychical structures have an overriding influence within the social: the psychic exists in an 'as yet to be determined extent' within social relations. This discontinuous relation is manifested in the structure of fantasy which, in as far as it involves the representation of a primordial absence, is linked to a universal structure of desire – a 'foundational' but not ahistorical fantasy (Brennan 1993: 22). Fantasies necessarily draw upon the socio-historical realm for their specific content, yet the immanence of the socio-historical within the content of fantasy cannot be established in any straightforward fashion. The effects of fantasy are not contained within the private sphere of the individual psyche but influence interaction with others in that they are constantly propelled into the social realm. In this way, psychic reality may be sustained, intensified or contradicted by its material context. Thus, as Brennan points out, it is ambiguous whether the fantasy of woman (as virgin-whore) would persist or fade into a 'pale myth' if it were not tied to concrete relations which disempower women and which literally 'passify' them (Brennan 1990: 131).[4]

Agency and lack

Despite the attempts of Brennan, Cornell and others to intro-
duce a greater sense of historicity into the psychoanalytic paradigm, these attempts remain limited by the primacy accorded
to the psyche, which always remains determining in the last
instance. The priority attributed to psychic dynamics forecloses
a full understanding of historical variation within society. In
Brennan's work, for example, the pre-eminence of psychic
dynamics over other social and political structures is evident in
so far as the former comprise the parameters of the social –
evident in the idea of a foundational fantasy – rather than vice
versa. That this causal priority could be reversed – that it is
the internalization of social norms that is constitutive of the
psyche rather than the other way round – or understood as
reciprocal is a possibility that is not seriously considered.

Thus, although Lacanian psychoanalysis seems to offer, in
theory, an explanation of the durability of hegemonic gender
norms without asserting their inevitability, there remains a
sense in which its structural account of gender formation
cannot accommodate easily a socio-historical emphasis on the
variable nature of subject formation. For example, although it
is stated that the symbolic realm is not an abstract system of
signification but a historically differentiated order, the primarily structural account of sexual differentiation tends towards
a form of acculturalism that obfuscates the variable and change-
able nature of systems of power. The primacy of *langue* over
parole in Lacan's concept of the symbolic forecloses an analysis
of the situated nature of discourse and of the attendant problems of struggles over meaning, power relations and practice.
In Fraser's words: 'the structuralist abstraction *langue* is troped
into a quasi divinity, a normative "symbolic order" whose power
to shape identities dwarfs to the point of extinction that of
mere historical institutions and practices' (Fraser 1997: 157).
The failure to consider how social power may be composed of
other norms and relations, which may reinforce or conflict
with patriarchy, means that Lacanian psychoanalysis provides
no way of explaining the variability of sexual identity, either

cross-culturally or in terms of cross-cutting identifications which exceed the binary frame of heterosexuality (Grosz 1990; Moore 1994). The extent to which socio-historical variability is negated is evident, for Butler, where homosexual identity is confined to the pre-social domain of the imaginary, thus 'preserving the heterosexism of culture through relegating homosexuality to the unrealizable life of passing fantasy' (Butler 1993a: 111).

The formalism of the Lacanian paradigm is compounded by its negativity, that is, the core assertion that identity is formed around a lack. The idea of an originary lack implies, at some level, that identity is illusory and it also permits the relation between the symbolic and the psyche to be construed in the uni-directional terms of imposition of the former upon the latter. The lack that forms the condition of possibility and impossibility of all speaking subjects is compounded for women by the inevitable assumption of a feminine identity which is primarily defined in relation to a phallocentric system of signification. Criticisms of the complicity of Lacan's theory with this phallocentrism – that it normalizes rather than challenges the subordination of the feminine – are partially rebutted by the argument that the assumption of sexual identity has a cost for all human subjects as 'speaking beings' in that the complexity of the child's early life is forced into the straitjacket of heterosexual polarity: 'The real lack is what the living being loses, that part of himself *qua* living being, in reproducing himself through the way of sex. This lack is real because it relates to something real, namely, that the living being, by being subject to sex, has fallen under the blow of individual death' (Lacan 1977c: 205). The phallus is a symbolic, not a literal, term, to which value accrues. Yet anatomical differences acquire significance in so far as the actual penis comes to figure in the representation of lack marking symbolic castration. The penis of the little boy lends itself to an approximation to or symbolization of the phallus. The problem, however, is that the penis is not the phallus and, therefore, the boy struggles to have the phallus. The little girl does not possess the penis which means that she has no means to represent her lack. Thus whilst both the position of the boy and of the girl to the phallus is problematic, the girl's position is more problematic because it is assigned a purely negative relation to the phallus (see Grosz 1990: 116). Woman's entry into the symbolic is defined, therefore, in terms of a double negativity or 'masquerade' in which the imposition of patriarchal dominance appears to be an inescapable cost of identity constitution. It is unclear how any position outside of the phallocentric matrix could be maintained; in other words, power is always already patriarchal. There emerges, therefore, an overdeterminism where the process of identity formation becomes necessary, invariant and unalterable (Leland 1992).

An effect of this privileging of the psyche over society is that the unconscious, *qua* lack, comes to stand in for an account of agency. Agency is elided with the disruptive effects of the unconscious upon seemingly certain social forms. There are difficulties, however, with the way in which psychoanalysis construes the unconscious or the Real as the invariant source of trauma or point of non-closure for any ideological or symbolic system. The concepts of the unconscious and the Real denote the contingency of any social formation in that they constitute a traumatic kernel which prevents its full institution. However, in as much as such concepts represent a self-identical dynamic that emerges in all social formations, the specific historicity or contingency of social systems is undercut. Butler remarks on the homogenizing effects of the idea of unconscious disruption in her critique of Slavoj Žižek's psychoanalytic formulation of the concept of ideology: 'the notion of a lack taken from psychoanalysis as that which secures the continency of *any* and *all* social formations is itself a presocial principle universalised at the cost of every consideration of power, sociality, culture, politics, which regulates the relative closure and openness of social practices' (Butler 1993a: 202). Explaining the non-closure of social systems through repeated reference to a self-identical principle forecloses a whole series of issues pertaining to the historicity of agency and change. One important connection that the invariant logic of this psychic remainder fails to establish is how such a negative source of disruption within the dominant may be sublimated or transmogrified into a more positive force underlying the emergence and creation of new social identities. Another issue that is not addressed is how the disruptive status of the unconscious may be thrown into doubt when there are unconscious attachments to subjection, rather than resistances; as Butler puts it: 'To thwart the injunction to produce a docile body is not the same as dismantling the injunction or changing the terms of subject constitution' (Butler 1997b: 88). In other words, the negative principle of unconscious disruption does not provide a sufficiently nuanced account of the varying modalities of agency and sociality.

A consequence of the substitution of a theory of agency by the self-identical principle of unconscious disruption is the implicit valorization of the pre-reflexive as a source of political resistance. For example, in *Volatile Bodies* Elizabeth Grosz claims that the ontological incompleteness of the body leads to a 'counterviolence of resistance', and yet such a short-circuited move occludes an analysis of the social relations mediating between the body and dominant norms. It is only through an examination of these mediatory relations that the notion of resistance is rendered meaningful in political terms, going beyond the narrow parameters of resistance defined only through reference to the individual psyche. As Simone de Beauvoir points out, the language of psychoanalysis suggests that the drama of the individual unfolds only within the self and this obscures the extent to which the individual's life and actions involve primarily a 'relation to the world' (1972: 80). The instability of corporeal identity may form the grounds from which a refashioning of gender norms arises, but to explain the emergence and impact of new practices and values upon realms beyond those of the individual necessitates the examination of attendant socio-cultural power relations. Analysis of the way in which certain subversive practices may get taken up and collectivized is important if resistance is to mean anything other than the truism that individuals do not reproduce social norms in a straightforward fashion. Thus, while the force of the psychoanalytic account of the instability of identity must be acknowledged, it is undermined by the extent to which a primarily psychic account of resistance to what Castoriadis has called the 'identitarian logic' of the symbolic order evacuates the social realm of any specificity. The psyche might well constitute the necessary grounds of some kinds of resistance to processes of normalization, but the idea does not explain sufficiently the specific mechanisms and efficacy of different types of agency.

The social in the psychic

Judith Butler (1997b) has recently tried to overcome the psychoanalytic foreclosure of a historical account of agency by reversing the causal privilege that the psychic is accorded in respect of the social. Unlike Brennan and Cornell, Butler presents not a case of presocial psychic structures propelling themselves into the social, but rather, following Foucault, a dynamic where the internalization of historically variable norms is formative of the psyche. Unlike Foucault, however, who underestimates the indeterminacy of the mechanisms of internalization, Butler argues that it is an uneven process whose dynamic is shaped by prevailing social and historical relations. It is this socially determined process of internalization which is constitutive of the split between psychic and social power (1997b: 19). At the same time, the dynamic temporality of the process of internalization means that the psyche is not reducible to the social: 'Just as the subject is derived from conditions of power that precede it, so the psychic operation of the norm is derived, though not mechanically or predictably, from prior social operations' (1997b: 21). Power turns back upon itself, producing the domain of the psyche which inheres within the social – evident in the way in which psychic phenomena circumscribe the domain of liveable sociality – but which is never prior to the social and is always vulnerable to historical change.

The force of Butler's sociocentric understanding of the formation of the psyche lies, in part, in its explanation of the non-correspondence between hegemonic gender norms and sexuality in terms other than presocial imaginary identifications which leave the symbolic intact as an immutable law. As we have seen, the formulation of lack as constitutive of identity renders Lacan's work vulnerable to the charge that it presupposes the subordination which it is intended to explain.

The psyche poses little resistance to entry into the symbolic because of its fundamentally negative character and also because the cost of defaulting on the symbolic is psychosis. Thus, the inevitability of the patriarchal symbolic is reinforced and a theory of agency undermined. Butler attempts to overcome this predominantly repressive account of the symbolic by reconfiguring the relation between psyche and society so that the latter does not lose determinate content. However, although the causal chain between psyche and society is inverted, ultimately Butler does not move beyond the essentially negative account of subject formation in Lacan and Foucault and, therefore, the concept of agency remains similarly underdeveloped. Agency remains primarily a strategy of displacement of constraining symbolic norms, rather than, in more active terms, an appropriation of cultural resources arising from the broader struggle 'for the social control of historicity' (Touraine 1977: 31).

The implicit tendency to elevate an invariant logic of resignification over a more explicitly political account of agency is evident in Butler's explanation of gender as melancholia where all forms of symbolic identification – heterosexual and homosexual – are achieved only at the cost of a certain forceclosure or melancholia, understood as a refused process of grieving. The relinquishment of the object of desire necessary to the formation of gender identity involves a loss which is never fully avowed by being melancholically incorporated into the ego. Thus, heterosexual identity is based on the abandonment of homosexual attachments which, because they cannot be grieved for, are preserved in the psyche as repudiated identifications. Conversely, rigid forms of homosexual identity can sometimes be based on a rejection of heterosexuality that is to some degree an identification with it, for example, the gay drag queen could be seen as an allegorization of an unavowed loss of the feminine object of desire. For Butler, it is important that this idea of melancholia be understood not as a psychic economy, but as part of the operations of regulatory social power which are contingently organized through certain kinds of foreclosure. Thus, to give expression to that grief is to acknowledge a loss which is denied, and to voice an anger which can result in political acts of resistance, for example the Names Project Quilt commemorating those who have died of AIDS (1997b: 148). Thus Butler's notion of the performative provides a way of investing psychic terms with a political force without losing sight, as social constructionism often does, of the instability of all forms of identification. Yet, although it provides a compelling explanation of the anger or desire that may underlie various forms of social protest, the idea of gender melancholia leaves unaddressed the mechanisms through which these psychic reserves are channelled into collective forms of activity. This would involve looking beyond the interface between psyche and social to consider the political as an effect of the shifting power relations between groups of social actors and between institutional and non-institutional structures. As it stands, the account of agency implied in the performative arises from the non-identity between psyche and society; however, given that this non-identity forms the condition of possibility of all identity, it cannot really explain the process of active appropriation that is required to explain action, particularly the types of action that result in the emergence of new social forms.

In sum, although social constructionist accounts of gender identity reject the determining force accorded to psychic formations in psychoanalysis, they often share an inherently negative conception of the symbolic as the realm of constraint which results in a valorization of any act of resignification as inherently radical. A consequence of this idea of the symbolic as repressive is that a concept of agency is confined to an invariant logic of displacement. Also not recognized is the extent to which the symbolic itself is composed of conflicting values and resources which may be actively appropriated by actors to institute new value systems and new forms of collective identity. The construal of the socio-symbolic order as a uniform realm of constraint disregards the innovative and dynamic nature of action by confining it to the relatively narrow idea of resistance. By locating the source of change in the permanent disjunction between the psyche and society, such constructionist accounts run the risk of replicating the psychoanalytic dehistoricization of the idea of agency. At the limit, notions of performance and resignification border on becoming self-identical principles which foreclose an analysis of the variable configuration of power relations underlying social action and change.

It is with regard to this difficulty, namely that the concept of unconscious disruption does not adequately explain agency and change within the socio-political realm, that the work of Cornelius Castoriadis is of interest. Elaborating on the idea of the creative nature of action from a psychoanalytic perspective, Castoriadis construes the relation between psyche and society as one of inherence where neither side is reducible to the other. The idea of inherence is implied in the Lacanian paradigm, but conceptual difficulties with the formulation of the internalization of phallocentric meaning pushes the idea of subject formation closer to a uni-directional model of determination. Castoriadis develops the idea of inherence through a reconceptualization of the imaginary as an originary capacity for figuration, rather than, *pace* Lacan, as a specular logic which imputes an illusory coherence to the subject. This reformulation of the imaginary as a capacity for 'presentification' yields a fuller account of the varied logic of the socio-symbolic realm and, as we shall see in the final sections, provides a more substantive account of the ontological grounds of the creative dimensions of agency.

Determinism and creativity

The point from which Castoriadis begins his reconceptualization of agency is a consideration of how the emergence of the new, *ex nihilo*, highlights limitations in the determinist models of action that prevail in Marxist theory. The central problem of the Marxist insistence on the primacy of economic structures is that it precludes an account of creative activity and an explanation of the constitutive role played by individuals in the formation and development of human society. By transposing the notion of creativity from the sphere of human activity to a property of the economic system, the Marxist theory of history does not in fact offer the explanation of praxis that it claims. The understanding of historical movement in terms of the unfolding of necessary stages relating to the contradiction between forces and relations of production yields a theory of social stasis rather than social change. Historical change is not the result of the inevitable realization of law-like tendencies, but rather of the '"self-awareness" and the activity of classes . . . [which] give rise to new, unpredetermined, and unpredeterminable elements' (Castoriadis 1987: 32). It is an explanation of the irregular, the unusual and the unanticipated that is precluded by the telos of the Marxian dialectic.

While Marxist philosophy partially acknowledges the unpredictable and creative aspects of human activity in the revolutionary moment, its determinist schema disregards the existence of creative elements in even the most rationalized forms of human activity. Castoriadis illustrates this point through a critique of the Marxist category of reification which, he claims, contrary to Marx's assertion at the beginning of *Capital*, can never be fully realized. If social relations were fully reified – that is, if all human relations were rendered thing-like and the dynamism of the social realm derived only from economic forces – the capitalist system would come to a standstill or collapse. It is the implicit, unseen creative activity of individuals that provides capitalism with its dynamism and flexibility. A factory in which the workers were 'mere cogs in the machine' or passive props of the system, unthinkingly carrying out the orders from management, would cease to function in a quarter of an hour. The final contradiction of capitalism resides in the extent to which the system's profound tendency towards reification is not realized by being continually countered by the creative activity of those it seeks to subject (Castoriadis 1987: 16).

All rational determination leaves outside of it an undetermined and non-rational remainder. And this remainder – of the unpredictable, the irregular – is as essential to any notion of social change as the ideas of necessity and regularity. In Castoriadis's view, any account of society must contain a notion of the non-causal as one of its essential moments. The non-causal element is a way of representing creative behaviour. Creative behaviour is understood not simply as unanticipated actions, but also as the positing of a new type of behaviour, as the *institution* of a new object or form, as 'an emergence or a production which cannot be deduced on the basis of a previous situation, as a conclusion that goes beyond the premises or as the positing of new premises' (1987: 44). In this way, historical being exceeds the brute demands of existence by providing new responses to the same situations or creating new situations. Like Ricoeur, Castoriadis argues that the recognition of a creative substrate to action should not be understood as a naive celebration of praxis. Creation does not necessarily signify goodness or the creation of positive values: 'Auschwitz and the Gulag are creations just as much as the Parthenon and the *Principia Mathematica*' (Castoriadis 1991: 3–4). Rather an emphasis on the creative dimensions of action highlights the shortcomings of the rationalist and determinist notions of agency that prevail in the social sciences (Joas 1996). History cannot be thought in accordance with such a determinist schema because it is the domain of creation.

The imaginary institution

Castoriadis connects the idea of the creativity of action to an explanation of the institution and reproduction of society through the radical and social imaginaries. The social imaginary is linked to the notion of creativity in so far as it is understood, at the level of collective social existence, as the faculty of presenting or positing things and relations that do not exist. This capacity to pose images *ex nihilo* suggests that society is inconceivable as the work or product of an individual or host of individuals, but is an ontological condition of the social realm itself. Thus Castoriadis also extends his notion of the imaginary to incorporate an explanation of the underpinning of the realm of the socio-historical in the psychic makeup of individuals. That is, the social imaginary has a structural homology in the radical imagination of the individual which has the capacity to posit or represent that which does not as yet exist.

In Castoriadis's view, psychoanalysis has a central weakness in that it cannot conceive of the psyche as radical imagination,

that is, as 'the emergence of representations or as representative flux not subject to determinacy' (1987: 274). Freudian
psychoanalysis partially recognizes the psyche as radical imagination, as the capacity to make representations *ex nihilo*.
Yet, although it accords a central role to dreams, phantasy, etc.,
it fails to take account fully of the constitutive nature of
the radical imagination in the formation of the psyche. Understood as a process of originary phantasmatization, the radical
imagination pre-exists and presides over every organization of
the drives, even the most primitive ones (1987: 286–7).

The extent to which psychoanalysis fails to capture the
constitutive role of the imagination is exemplified in Lacan's
concept of the imaginary. The crux of Castoriadis's objection
is the extent to which Lacan reduces the plenitude of the
imaginary to the flatness of the specular structure. The imaginary is illusory to the extent that it conceals or sutures a
fundamental lack in the subject. From the age of six months,
the human infant is able to recognize and respond to its own
image in the mirror. The child's assumption of its specular
image prefigures the paradoxical nature of the subsequent formation of the subject in language – the symbolic realm. On
the one hand, the specular image gives the child its first sense
of coherent identity – it anticipates the maturation of the
adult's power as subject. On the other hand, the image is a
'mirage' because it artificially freezes and unifies the child's
lack of motor coordination and anatomical incompleteness into
a premature notion of the self. Further, in as much as identity
is only given to the infant through the exteriority of the mirror
(or the gaze of the mother), it is founded on a misrecognition
because it itself is divided by the exterior presence of an other
through which it is constituted. The mirror stage is imaginary,
then, because it is based on the misrecognition of the fragmented self as autonomous: 'the *mirror stage* is a drama whose
internal thrust is precipitated from insufficiency to anticipation – and which manufactures for the subject . . . the succession of phantasies that extends from a fragmented body-image
to a form of its totality' (Lacan 1977a: 4). Subsequently this
lack is connected to the impossibility of acquiring stable identity within the symbolic order. For Lacan, then, the imaginary

is an illusory or negative moment because it covers up an originary rift or lack in the subject.

Castoriadis criticizes this notion of the imaginary as an illusory suturing of lack because its specular logic is unable to explain why it is that the infant is first impelled to identify, invest and recognize itself in the mirror. Prior to the specular moment of reflection, the mirror itself must be invested with desire: 'The imaginary does not come from the image in the mirror or from the gaze of the other. Instead, the "mirror" itself and its possibility, and the other as mirror, are the works of the imaginary, which is creation *ex nihilo*' (1987: 3). The anterior investment of the mirror signals the work of the radical imaginary which is able to invest, create and represent *ex nihilo*. It is possible to discern the work of the radical imagination in the way in which the somatic objects are taken up and invested.[5] The construal of the lacking object as desirable is an *anaclisis*, a psychical creation of the radical imagination. The imaginary is not, therefore, a specular structure which seeks to conceal lack, but an originary capacity of figuration or presentification. It is a mode of being of the psyche, a 'representing-representation' to which nothing is missing, in which there is no distinction between representation, intuition and affect, and from which emerges phantasy and alteration of phantasy (Castoriadis 1987: 290). Echoing the definition of the social imaginary as the capacity to create the new *ex nihilo*, the radical imagination, at the level of the individual unconscious, 'brings itself into being, makes be that which exists nowhere else and which, for us, is the condition for anything at all to be able to exist' (1987: 292).

In the original, undifferentiated state of 'auto-cathexis' associated with the radical imaginary where the psyche has not yet undergone the breakup imposed upon it by the object, the other and its own body, the subject is in a state of what Castoriadis calls 'monadic madness'. In this state, the psyche knows no boundaries: it is in an unceasing condition of representative flux. The subsequent evolution of the subject is the history of the psyche's socialization, that is to say, the process through which the subject is instituted as an individual within the socio-historical realm. It is only the institution of

Psyche and Society

society, proceeding from the social imaginary, that can limit the radical imagination of the psyche, call it out of its monadic madness and bring reality into being for it (1987: 309). The drawing out of the individual through the social imaginary takes the form of 'sublimation'. This process of sublimation is not an organic process but takes the form of a 'violent breakup' in which the psyche takes up the socially instituted forms or significations (*eide*): 'the appropriation of the social by the psyche through the constitution of an interface – between the private world and the public or common world' (1987: 312).

Although the social institution of the individual is necessary to bring the subject out of monadic madness, the institution can never completely absorb the psyche in so far as it is radical imagination. The relation between society and the psyche is inseparable and irreducible and forms a positive condition of the existence and functioning of society: 'The constitution of the social individual does not and cannot abolish the psyche's creativity, its perpetual alteration, the representative flux as the continuous emergence of other representations' (1987: 320–1). The representative flux that precedes ensemblist or identarian thought and the orthodox social vision imposed upon it gives, in theory, each individual access to what escapes the schemata of identity. The uninterrupted surging of representative flux is the capacity to create the new or imagine things that do not as yet exist (1987: 323). It is this representative flux which permits the emergence of the other in and through the positing of images and figures. This representative flux forms a type of immanent transcendence – a passage to the other or to the new in the socio-historical (1987: 329–31).

Inherence and agency

Castoriadis's concept of the radical imaginary shares the destabilizing force of the psychoanalytic category of the unconscious; the resistance of the representative flux of the imaginary to full incorporation into the symbolic realm attests to the unfinished nature of all social identity. However, distinct from the symbolic determinism of the Lacanian paradigm, Castoriadis formulates the relation between the radical and social imaginaries in terms of a generative bond of inherence. The notion of inherence, or leaning on, implies a relation of con-substantiality or interdependence where each side is implicated in but not reducible to the other (1987: 112). Crucially, it cannot be characterized as determination or dependence, freedom or alientation.[6] The configuration of the connection between psyche and society in terms of a generative relation of inherence explains the emergence of agency more easily than the rather top-heavy accounts of symbolic construction offered in the negative paradigm of subjectification.

The essentially negative notion of subjectification formed around a lack pushes the relation between the symbolic order and the unconscious into a uni-directional dynamic of deter-mination, although a generative capacity may be implied. The relation between the two realms is construed primarily in negat-ive terms as the internalization or introjection of the constraints of a phallocentric symbolic order (Laplanche and Pontalis 1973: 229–30). This results in an aporetic conception of the sym-bolic order as both monolithic and illusory. On the one hand, by suggesting that identity receives its form from the imposi-tion of symbolic order upon an originary lack, Lacan diminishes the principle of non-identity that the unconscious represents and slides towards a concept of the symbolic as invariant and uniform. In Castoriadis's view, if extralinguistic reality were simply amorphous clay that received its form entirely from within thought, there could be no perception: 'There is no perception if there is no representative flux . . . A subject that would have *only* perception would have *no* perception: it would be completely swallowed up by "things", flattened up against them, crushed against the world, incapable of shifting its gaze and so just as incapable of fixing it on the world' (Castoriadis 1987: 336).

The other side of the aporia is that the negative account of identity that Lacan's model yields tends to devalue concrete socio-historical identities in favour of an abstract notion of all identity as an imaginary unity. This results in a fetishization of the unconscious as a source of some, as yet, unexpressed identity. This is evident, for example, in certain feminist appropriations of Lacan's work. For example, Julia Kristeva's idea of the destabilizing implications of the semiotic and the abject for the symbolic subject lacks a notion of mediation to explain how such pre-Oedipal or inchoate forces may have an emancipatory impact on social practices. In the absence of any mediatory notion of political agency, Kristeva's work remains in a 'bad infinity', oscillating between the moments of 'structure and anti-structure' (Fraser 1997: 163). As Castoriadis puts it:

> If 'truth' is altogether on the side of the unconscious, and if all 'knowledge' is mere deception, what importance can the subjects's words have ... If the person is in fact nothing but *persona*, a mask, and if behind this *persona* he is nobody ... then surely the best way of leading the subject to the 'truth' is in fact to leave him to stew in his own juice? (1984: 57)

In short, in Lacan, the symbolic is both all-powerful and also devoid of substantive content, and this paradox hinders the formulation of an adequate account of historical practice and agency.

The subject to become subject must necessarily introject the uniform, repressive law of the father. The essential passivity of the subject that this assumes can lead to a uni-directional dynamic which yields, at best, a residually negative account of agency and, at worst, denies agency altogether. Trapped within the Moebius loop of lack–repetition–death, terms such as agency and praxis are foreign to the Lacanian framework: 'the life of the subject can never be anything more than a continual voyage round and round the single surface of a Moebius strip, whose possible varieties have been fixed, once and for all ... by "structure"' (Castoriadis 1984: 58). The subject is a submissive entity trapped beneath the oppressive weight of political and social institutions that maintain their force at the level of the psyche. The notions of creativity, agency and change are excluded from the outset. Lacanian psychoanalysis misses this imaginative and active aspect of social action because of the emphasis it places on the repressive inscription of the individual which is forced on the imaginary with entry into the

socio-symbolic order: 'these standpoints fail to accord due recognition to the active dimensions of subjecthood; to the point
that ideological and social fields are rewritten and changed
within the indeterminacy of subjectivity' (Elliott 1992: 243).

By conceptualizing the relation between psyche and society in terms of an *inherence*, Castoriadis suggests a model of
subjectification that involves more than submission to the law
of the symbolic. It explains how the subject is invested with an
active disposition towards the world. The idea of unconscious
as lack tells us about the impossibility of identity rather than
the motivational basis for change or self-alteration. By attri-
buting a positivity to pre-linguistic being as radical flux,
Castoriadis partially overcomes this problem because the relation between the social and the psychic becomes one of a
mutual realization, rather than introjection of a repressive law.
A logic of determination – of the social by the psychic or vice
versa – is replaced with the idea of mutual inherence where,
on the one hand, the realm of the imaginary is not dictated by
'real' factors: the real is always already symbolized (1987: 123–
4). On the other hand, the social imaginary is not completely
free in the sense that it necessarily 'leans on' corporeality to
institute symbolization (1987: 127). The radical imaginary is
an irreducible psychic structure, but it receives its content and
intelligibility from being projected out into the social realm.
Thus it might be an irreducible structure, but it is not an
invariant one in so far as the symbolic is infinitely varied.

The parallel between the representative flux of the radical
and social imaginary suggests that there cannot simply be chaos
or lack prior to figuration. If there were no inherence between
psyche and society, then it is not clear where a principle of
non-identity would emerge from, since the break between
being and thought would be absolute (Gasché 1994). This is
a problem for Habermas, for example, who by reducing the
unconscious or pre-linguistic inner nature to the linguistic cir-
cle of intersubjectivity loses any notion of radical non-identity
resulting in an impoverished notion of individuation (Whitebook
1996: 185–6). This does not imply that it is possible to discern
being in itself (*Ding an sich*); rather it is the inherence of radical
and social imaginary that forms the 'logical and ontological'

grounds of the interweaving of identity and non-identity within the social realm (Castoriadis 1987: 336). It should be noted that Castoriadis's formulation of the notion of inherence is not unambiguous; there are points at which the idea of con-substantiality is replaced with an assertion of radical alterity. Here, Castoriadis seems to imply that the representative flux of the radical imaginary is absolutely heterogeneous to the social and that the process of sublimation represents a 'violent break, forced by its "relation" to others, more precisely, by the invasion of others as others' (1987: 301). However, as Joel Whitebook points out, the assertion of the radical otherness of the monadic core of the psyche to the social undermines the notion of inherence, for it would mean that the 'socialization process would not simply be violent, it would be impossible' (Whitebook 1996: 180). In order to sustain the relation of inherence, therefore, it would seem reasonable to argue, as Castoriadis does elsewhere, that experience or being must be understood as having a pre-linguistic nature in that it is amen-able to figuration and organization: 'the object . . . is in some sense *organizable*' (Whitebook 1996: 174).

The thematization of the inherence of the radical and social imaginaries around the idea of a primary capacity for presentification, rather than lack, offers a more compelling account of the ontological basis of certain aspects of agency. The originary capacity for figuration explains why it is that individuals are motivated to act in creative or unanticipated ways. How it is that, within the constraints of a prevailing social order, individuals may respond to problems and difficulties through the institution of new practices. In the case of gender identity, it explains why women as historical subjects are not crushed by the constraints of a phallocentric order but have been able to act autonomously within its interstices. Drawing heavily upon Castoriadis's work, Anthony Elliott argues, for example, that a notion of imagination proceeding from the creative flux of the unconscious is essential to an explanation of agency in a post-traditional social order. The uncertain and complex nature of identities and practices in a detraditionalized society invokes heightened levels of reflexivity on the part of individual actors. Individuals must partly respond in an open and innovative fashion to social complexity and difference if they are to create meaningful and coherent existences from the contingent flux of the world. This notion of creative re-flexivity or toleration for the irreconcilable and ambivalent that the idea of agency often presupposes cannot easily be derived from a paradigm which emphasizes the passivity of the subject and a relation to the other based on a refusal of differ-ence. For example, Castoriadis argues that the changing situation of women's social role is a prime example of the creative aspects latent in even the most mundane and unreflective types of action: 'it has been carried out collectively, anonymously, daily, by women themselves, without their even explicitly representing to themselves its goals' (Castoriadis 1991: 205). Reformulating the idea of agency in these terms also runs against theories of postmodernity which posit, to varying degrees, a decomposition of the unitary subject as an effect of the pluralizing and fragmenting tendencies operating upon the social realm. Against such claims, it is surely correct to argue that social instability leads to an intensification of agency rather than its diminution. In short, it is not necessary to accept all aspects of the detraditionalization thesis in order to see that an understanding of the creative elements inherent to agency are important in explaining how men and women negotiate the uncertainties thrown up by processes of gender restructuring.

Instituting–instituted

It is not only the thematization of a relation of inherence between the realms of the psyche and the symbolic that ex-plains the motivational basis of agency, but also Castoriadis's replacement of a linguistic or discursive concept of the sym-bolic with the sociocentric category of the social imaginary. The social imaginary encompasses the symbolic, but it is un-derstood as a broader entity. It is the domain in which differ-ent codes – the symbolic, the ideological, the mythical – are interwoven, and is characterized by an oscillation between the tendencies to impose order and to self-alteration; the dialectic of the *instituting–instituted*. The generative dynamic of the

instituting–instituted checks the tendency to explain subjectification in terms of a symbolic determinism, thereby offering
a way of thinking of the creative aspects to agency.

The recognition of an irreducibly creative moment in social
activity leads Castoriadis to his definition of the social world
or socio-historical realm as the instituting–instituted. This is
to say that society is both the product of instituting human
activity or creative human praxis and, at the same time, the
materialized institutions of socio-historical creation acquire
an autonomy of their own, appearing independent and self-
instituted, thereby exerting a determining force upon human
activity. There is, therefore, always a gap between society as
instituting and that which is instituted; this gap is not something negative but one of the 'expressions of the creative nature
of history'. It is this disjunction that prevents society from ever
being fully formed or fixed and signifies an indeterminacy in
the socio-historical domain which means that society always
contains more than it presents.

Everything in the socio-historical world is tied to the symbolic realm which forms part of the social imaginary. Institutions can only exist if they are part of a symbolic network
although they are not reducible to it. To be meaningful, all
social relations must pass through symbolization: '"real social
relations" . . . are always *instituted* . . . because they have been
posited as universal, symbolized and sanctioned ways of doing
things' (1987: 124). The centrality of symbolization in social
life means that societies cannot be understood as functional
systems because they are permeated with meanings which are
not dictated by real factors. For example, any society needs to
eat and to produce children in order to survive. However, beyond this brute necessity, the process of human reproduction
is carried out in an infinite variety of ways. There is no un-
adorned fact of reproduction that precedes social meaning;
rather facts only acquire meaning within the symbolic imaginary
that invests the real with significance (1987: 145). The symbolic
refers to the way in which aspects of social life are invested
with meaning which is not solely dictated by the functional
demands of the real. For example, God or the nation are imaginary significations which have no referent: both these ideas

are neither perceived (real), nor thought (rational), and yet they are ordering principles of much social action.

Although all instituted social relations are inextricably linked to symbolization, they are not reducible to it. This introduces a key distinction from the negative paradigm, namely the conflation upwards where the socio-historical domain is subsumed within the symbolic which, in turn, is subsumed within the linguistic order. This linguistic reduction narrowly equates questions of subjectification and agency with positionality in language. Castoriadis introduces a number of distinctions to avoid this conflation of the realm of the socio-historical with that of the symbolic. Although language is a primary form of symbolization, it is not the only form: there are certain institutional forms – a pay cheque, a legal decision, a hangman's act – which although symbolic do not necessarily pass directly through language (1987: 117). More importantly, however, the symbolic and the social imaginary are distinct. Symbolism assumes the capacity of positing a permanent connection between two terms in such a way that one 'represents' the other. The relation between a signification and its supports (images and figures) is the only precise sense that can be attached to the term symbolic (1987: 238). In this respect, the social imaginary must pass through the symbolic in order to express itself. However, the symbolic cannot exist without the social imaginary understood as the prior capacity to 'see in a thing what it is not, to see it other than it is' (1987: 127). Thus, while the symbolic is the realm of instituted meaning, the social imaginary exceeds it in that it is the realm of the instituted and instituting; it is the 'invisible cement holding together this endless collection of real, rational and symbolic odds and ends that constitute every society' (1987: 143). The imaginary is that which defines social identity, that which gives a specific orientation to every institutional system. It gives unity to an incalculable number of gestures, investing the world with meaning, content and style, thereby ensuring that the total world given to a particular society is apprehended in a certain way.

In the negative paradigm, it is the subsumption of social life into the symbolic and the conceptualization of the symbolic only as the realm of instituted phallocentric meaning that results in a reification of gender identity. The modelling of the symbolic around *langue* does not recognize sufficiently the sociocentric nature of language – the symbolic realm cannot be reduced to gendered codes alone – and excludes, therefore, any principle of internal differentiation. Nor does it adequately recognize the inherent unevenness of symbolic codes evident in, say, the difference between the ideas of the ideological and the symbolic (Benhabib 1995: 109–10). Language in the symbolic realm becomes a closed system in which the phallus seems to control meaning, illustrated, for example, in Lacan's claim that 'the woman is engaged in an order of exchange in which she is an object; indeed, this is what causes the fundamentally conflictual character of her position – I would say *without exit*. The symbolic order literally submerges and transcends her' (quoted in Leland 1992: 123). Any disruption to the symbolic system comes from outside, from the self-identical dissonance between the psyche and the symbolic (*jouissance*, unconscious), but it is not understood as immanent to the symbolic itself.[7] Thus, the instability of all social meanings is frozen by being subsumed within an abstract linguistic order: 'symbols in fact envelop the life of man in a network so total . . . that they bring to his birth . . . the shape of his destiny' (Lacan 1977b: 68).

In contrast, Castoriadis's idea of the dialogic interaction between the instituting and instituted allows him to posit the instability of meaning in thoroughly social terms as a process of referral or a 'magma of significations'. The imposition of order (through the idea of heteronomy) effected within the social imaginary is at odds with the capacity for self-alteration. This dialectic of the instituting and instituted generates an endless process of referral in which the institution of a certain set of primary significations begets further secondary significations. Thus the idea that God created the world in seven days is part of the central imaginary of Mosaic religion. However, this proliferates into secondary imaginaries, such as the sanctification of the week which itself has innumerable consequences, such as 'the level of the rate of surplus-value, the frequency curve of sexual intercourse in Christian societies showing a periodic maximum every seven days, and the mortal boredom of English Sundays' (1987: 129). The social imaginary manifests itself through an indefinite show of interminable referrals to something 'other than': each referral leads to a new referral and so on. Thus the institution of society involves the institution of a magma of significations: 'the magma never ceases to move, to swell and to subside ... it is because the magma is such, that man can move himself and create in and through language' (1987: 244). It is this understanding of the social imaginary as a limitless skein of referrals that marks the difference with conceptions of the symbolic as an abstract system of signification. The openness of language does not derive only from the relational character of the signifier, but also from the necessarily socio-historical character of language. It is this instability in signification which permits the creation of the new in and through language: an impossibility if language were a completely determined code or the symbolic an apparently incontestable order. Indeed, this idea of a magma of infinite significations is the condition of possibility of any identity fixation since the latter can only emerge as such against the background of instability or non-identity.

Oedipus and sublimation

The idea of a magma of signification yields a less overwhelmingly negative account of the instauration of feminine identity. To be a woman is to be situated partially within dominant norms of femininity, but it also involves being located simultaneously along other vectors of power. The historical variability of definitions of femininity means that they carry within them reference to other definitions of womanhood and personhood which do not necessarily overlap seamlessly. Castoriadis's idea of the social imaginary provides a way of conceptualizing multiple subjectivity and a phenomenon, noted by Godelier, namely that around any social relation there exists a series of more or less elaborated other possible relations which traverse and counter it: 'a social relation cannot begin to exist really or be transformed without there arising contemporaneously other possible social forms which far from being inert work continually and act in it and on it' (Godelier 1984: 171). To be instituted as a woman is to be located in a series of social roles which refer to other roles, thus preventing fixation in any one position. It is such a process of referral that Bridget Riley alludes to when she argues that there cannot be a separate history of women's experience because it is always implicated within the development of more general legal, political and medical categories such as personhood, citizenship, the body and so forth.

The idea of the social imaginary as an endless skein of significations underlines more clearly than concepts of the phallocentric symbolic order the historically variable nature of gender subordination. For example, rather than being understood as a universal and invariant structure, the Oedipus complex can be said to be grounded in culturally and historically specific forms of praxis. From historical and cross-cultural perspectives, many commentators have cast doubt on the understanding of Oedipus as a universal necessity, rather than as a psychological abstraction from a specific configuration of Western familial relations (e.g. Fanon 1968: 152). This does not preclude an explanation of certain constant dimensions to gender oppression, but it does demand that such continuities are placed in the context of the specific social relations that sustain them. As Leland says: 'given that the social relations of male domination vary in different societies and in different historical periods as well as across class and ethnic lines, explanations of women's psychological oppression that focus on only one type of social relation . . . risk being oversimplified or reductionistic' (Leland 1992: 120; see also Moore 1994: 42–8). If internalized oppression is understood as based in historically specific institutions and practices, then a space for indetermination and agency is opened up. In Castoriadis, rather than being seen as an inescapable cost of the assumption of subjectivity, the origins of the negative status of femininity are located in the social imaginary. In other words, oppression is regarded not as a psychological inevitability, but as the effect of historical relations. This is illustrated in Castoriadis's socialized concept of sublimation, which tends to focus not so much on the intrasubjective dynamics of the individual psyche but on intersubjective relations of association and conflict.

Sublimation is the process by means of which the psyche is forced to replace its 'own' or 'private objects' of cathexis with objects which exist and have value in and through their social institution. Out of these it creates for itself 'causes, means or supports of pleasure' (1987: 312). For Castoriadis, sublimation is a process that is eminently social rather than individual. Rather than the drives being sublimated as objects that have meaning only for the individual, sublimation involves the establishment of a 'non-empty' intersection between the private and the public world which conforms to the requirements posited by the social institution (1987: 318). For the subject, objects no longer exist; instead, things and individuals: no longer private signs and words but a public language. The socio-historical institution of the subject is, for Castoriadis, one of the blind spots of psychoanalysis, which cannot adequately explain 'the transformation of the psychical monad into the social individual for whom there exists other individuals, objects, a world, a society, institutions – things none of which, originally, has meaning or existence for the psyche' (1987: 274). It is the institution of society which renders obligatory for the innumerable individuals of society particular objects of sublimation to the exclusion of others. Society can exist only to the extent that the objects of sublimation are at once 'typical, categorized *and* mutually complementary' (1987: 318).

The socio-historical inflexion given to the notion of sublimation explains how individuals are fitted into dissimilar roles in different societies. The understanding of Oedipus as a universal psychological structure precludes an adequate account of the role played by history in the socialization of the individual; its reliance on archetypal figures cannot explain the infinite variation and incommensurability of social roles (1987: 316). Oedipus obscures an understanding of meaning as a socio-historical phenomenon by tying it too closely to the figure of the father, whether it be literally or symbolically understood. By locating socialization in the system of signification that far exceeds the institution of the family, Castoriadis offers an explanation of how social roles may be historically variable and culturally specific. To be instituted as a capitalist does not

simply involve a psychic investment in certain relations with
money and machines, a sublimation of the anal drive, for example. The role of the capitalist is far too complex to be
simply a psychic creation. Rather, it involves a process of investment in the socially instituted role of the capitalist which
is caught up in a web of second-order institutions, categories
and meanings: 'Being a capitalist is investing this specific object, which can exist only as a social institution; the enterprise
as the complex arrangement of men and machines, implying
an indefinite number of other institutions and processes outside of the enterprise itself' (1987: 320). If this role did not
exist socially then this investment would be no more than a
fantasy or a psychosis. Thus, no psychic drive can predispose a
child in Athens or Rome to become president of General
Motors, just as no child in New York or Paris would wish to
become a pharaoh or a shaman except to the degree that this
rendered her psychotic.

If, in an analogous fashion, the instauration of feminine identity is understood as an effect of the social imaginary, then the
imbrication of gender with other structures of power can be
thought. The psychoanalytic privileging of gender as an originary
structure can be undone by thinking of the interarticulation of
structures of race, class and gender evident, for example, in
the racializing of class differences and and sexualizing of racial
stereotypes documented in work on colonial and post-colonial
identity (e.g. McClintock 1995; Pellegrini 1997). In this way, not
only can the social specificity of gender oppression be better
understood, but also the restriction of a concept of women's
agency by a return to an inevitable gender binary is circumvented.

Autonomy

By conceptualizing sublimation as an effect of the social-
imaginary, Castoriadis shows how the individual is a creation
not just of the psyche but of socio-historical forces. This socialized understanding of the individual as a collective category
suggests in turn a revised understanding of the concept of
autonomy. In the previous chapter we saw how the feminist

critique of the disembedded and disembodied subject of patriarchy can lead to a rejection of abstract thought in general. The counter-insistence on the situated nature of subjectivity can result, however, in an impasse in the conceptualization of agency in so far as the latter necessarily involves a partial transcendence of its conditions of emergence. Castoriadis's reconfiguration of the individual as a social creation suggests an analogous reformulation of autonomy, not as a self-enclosed state, but as an active–passive relation with the other. By orienting the idea of autonomy away from intrasubjective tensions, its intersubjective dimensions are highlighted and can be connected to social dynamics of affiliation and struggle.

Feminist psychoanalysis, particularly object relations theory, has developed a strong critique of the concept of autonomy as a masculine illusion of self-containment based on a denial of the relational nature of the self which is paradigmatically expressed in the mother–child dyad. Aware that such arguments risk inverting, rather than dissolving, the opposition between masculinity and femininity, certain feminists have attempted to reconstruct the relation of autonomy and dependence. For example, Jessica Benjamin argues that for feminist politics to progress it must break down the logic which polarizes and sexualizes the distinction between transcendence and immanence, or between the desire for autonomy and the recognition of one's dependence on others: 'Contrary to appearance, dependence and independence are not opposed . . . our politics must find a form of transcendence which does not repudiate immanence, the ties that give and maintain life' (Benjamin 1982: 153). Yet Benjamin elaborates her reworked concept of autonomy through the idea of the nurturing maternal bond: 'what is nurturance if not the pleasure in the other's growth?' (Benjamin 1978: 51). While Benjamin is right to question the idea of autonomy as a state of hermetic self-sufficiency, her reworking of the concept through a romanticized notion of motherhood is problematic. Rather than mediating the sexualized dualism of autonomy and dependence, she simply reframes it by arguing for the compatibility of a traditional conception of motherhood with encouragement to individuation (Johnson 1988: 22). What this work fails to do is to reconstruct, in non-naturalistic terms, an idea of autonomy as central to an understanding of agency. By construing women's agency always within a relational and often an implicitly maternal frame, the varied and changing nature of women's social experience is disregarded.

Castoriadis's thought recasts the idea of autonomy within the instituting–instituted dynamic of the social imaginary so that the opposition of monadic versus relational conceptions of the self is bypassed. Alienation occurs when the dialectic of the instituting–instituted becomes distorted so that the realization that society is a product of praxis is occluded in what Adorno has called the 'priority of the objective' (Benhabib 1986: 214).[8] On the level of the individual, alienation can be understood as heteronomy or submission to the discourse of the 'law of the Other'. Complete heteronomy or alienation is never possible in the sense that the self is totally effaced by the discourse of the Other. Equally, there cannot be an unconditional discourse of the self, that is, complete autonomy. The subject is not a self-sustaining monad, choosing its content in a pure act of will: 'Autonomy is ... not a clarification without remainder nor is it the total elimination of the discourse of the Other' (Castoriadis 1987: 104). The form or content of subjectivity is always necessarily given to us from our cultural context and, in so far as this is the case, the other is always present in the discourse of the self. Autonomy involves, therefore, the establishment of another relation between the discourse of the Other and the subject's discourse, a relation of activity–passivity where the subject critically reflects upon the relation between the self and the imaginary relations in which she is situated. The content of the self neither belongs to the subject nor to the other; rather there is a 'produced and productive union' of the self and the other, in Castoriadis's words, a 'continuous and continually actualizable possibility of regarding, objectifying, setting at a distance, detaching and finally transforming the discourse of the Other into the discourse of the subject' (1987: 105). In sum, autonomy of the self involves a form of 'self-limitation' revolving around the internalization of the necessity of laws and the possibility of putting those laws into question (1991: 173).

Castoriadis's understanding of autonomy as an active–passive relation between self and other suggests a way in which the concept may be incorporated into an understanding of gender identity and agency. As a relation in which the other is always present, autonomy cannot be conceptualized as a moment of pure subjectivity; rather it leads to a broader notion of sociality and politics (1987: 107). The relation with the other is conceived simultaneously as connection to the autonomized meanings of the social and as intersubjectivity, in so far as the latter is mediated by the former. In other words, the relation with the other involves both *extended* and immediate intersubjective relations and as such it necessarily leads to the social: 'if autonomy is the relation in which others are always present as the otherness *and* as the self-ness of the subject, then autonomy can be conceived of . . . only as a social problem and as a social relation' (1987: 108). Thus it is not possible to want autonomy, on an individual level, without wanting it for others and, therefore, its realization cannot be conceived of in its full scope except as a collective enterprise.

The definition of autonomy as involving both immediate and extended intersubjective relations contrasts with the tendency within object relations theory to understand intersubjectivity primarily through immediate familial relations. When the family is understood primarily as preceding broader social relations, this results in the confinement of agency to the terms of a naturalized sexual difference where masculinity is seen as transcendence and femininity as immanence. In particular, women's agency is delimited by a highly normative notion of the maternal function. When the family is understood as an effect of sociation whose relations are invested with meaning by the social imaginary, then the idea of autonomous agency is released from the logic that counterposes a masculine will to transcendence against a feminine will to connection. As an active–passive relation with the other which transcends the privatized unit of the family, autonomy is present to varying degrees in all action. It highlights the importance of rethinking relations of autonomy and subordination within the process of gender restructuring. If economic and social transformations are forcing a demassification of sexual division resulting in more complex and internally differentiated patterns of gender inequality, then relations of autonomy and dependence have to be rethought.

Conclusion

Castoriadis's reframing of the relation between psyche and society in terms of the irreducibly creative character of action permits the introduction of a greater sense of historicity into a psychoanalytic account of subject formation and agency. The concept of the radical imaginary as an originary capacity for figuration and the reconfiguring of the relation between psyche and society as one of inherence provides a more active notion of agency than the negative Lacanian paradigm. In particular, the overwhelming negativity that appears to be the inescapable cost of assuming feminine identity in Lacan is bypassed. Castoriadis's thought opens up a theoretical space for a more variable concept of agency in which to examine the historical practices of men and women without the foreclosure that a return to an inevitable sexual division provokes. The emphasis on the social specificity of gendered practices is facilitated further by the substitution of the linguistic concept of the symbolic with the idea of the social imaginary. The latter category allows the institution of gender inequalities to be understood as the work of social rather than psychic structures. Oedipus is no longer conceptualized as a universal necessity, but as a psychological correlate of intimate relations within the West. The characterization of the social imaginary as a dialectic between the imposition of order and self-alteration also presents a renewed understanding of autonomy not as a monadic state of self-transparency but as an active–passive relation with the other. In this way, the concept of autonomy is connected to broader social relations of affiliation and struggle. The idea of the creative and autonomous dimensions to agency explains certain innovative and unexpected features in the responses of men and women to shifts within gender relations that are unleashed by the detraditionalizing tendencies in late-capitalist societies.

5

GENDER AND CHANGE: CONCLUDING REMARKS

Feminist ideas of change

The question of agency inevitably raises the broader issue of change. An account of subjectification oriented to explaining the creative dimensions of agency ought to contribute to an understanding of change within gender relations. I have claimed that the expanded concept of agency that emerges from a generative account of subject formation provides a useful perspective from which to examine aspects to the restructuring of gender relations. The negative paradigm of subjectification provides too limited a description of the agent's capacities and this confines the analysis of change to the dichotomous logic of domination and resistance. A broader notion of agency as the subject's capability to deal with difference or otherness in terms other than exclusion or denial ultimately leads to a less dichotomous understanding of change within gender relations as discontinuous and uneven.

At the moment, two opposing conceptions of change seem to dominate feminist theory. On the one hand, there is the absolutization of change that emerges in work on the symbolic construction of the subject which tends to impute an inherently radical status to the indeterminacy of meaning systems. The fetishization of symbolic indeterminacy fails to accommodate adequately notions of structural and institutional inflexibility and can result in naive accounts of the transformatory

potential of libidinal practices. The instability of symbolic structures may form a necessary condition for the transformation of
social practices, but it is not a sufficient guarantor of change.
On the other hand, there are the more cautious materialist
accounts of change which assert that if gender relations are
transforming at all then it is in a gradual and complex fashion
where the emergence of new forms of autonomy coincides
with new forms of dependency and subordination. Thus, the
emphasis within symbolic feminism on the performative instabilities within gender norms is countered by the materialist
stress on the regular and predictable features of gender relations: 'while gender relations could potentially take an infinite
number of forms, in actuality there are some widely repeated
features' (Walby 1990: 16).

In many respects, the materialist feminist disaggregation of
univocal concepts of patriarchal domination to examine the
interrelations between distinct gender regimes provides a useful way of addressing the uneven and dispersed nature of transformation in gender relations. Against rather undifferentiated
ideas of symbolic indeterminacy, a multi-level understanding
of change unfolds. The sociologist Janet Saltzman Chafetz
(1990) argues, for example, that if the depth and pervasive-
ness of change within gender norms is to be assessed it must
be examined on the three levels of micro, mezzo and macro,
although the boundaries between the three domains are not
clear. Micro-level changes refer to intrapsychic phenomena as
they are affected by social and cultural factors and to face-to-
face interactions between individuals especially within dyads
and small groups. For gender sociologists, the family constitutes the most important micro-level institution. Mezzo-level
changes denote shifts within organizational structures, com-
munities and racial and ethnic groups and so forth. Macro-
level changes typically refer to society-wide phenomena, such
as economic and political systems, class and gender stratification (Saltzman Chafetz 1990: 14). Analysis of the interplay
between the different levels of change is important if the uneven effects of gender restructuring are to be recognized and if
voluntarist and culturally determinist theories of agency and
transformation are to be avoided. Although symbolic accounts

of subject formation explicitly reject voluntarist interpretations of the ways in which it is possible to refashion gender identities, this is often undercut by the attenuated account of agency evident, for example, in the problematic distinction between the ideas of the performative and the performance (Lloyd 1999: 203). It is also undermined by the failure to situate symbolic forms in material relations.

Against voluntarist models of change, Saltzman Chafetz claims that if change in gender norms is to be substantial and lasting it must flow from macro to micro levels: 'theory should identify the most likely sources of unintentional change, and the processes by which the gender system is affected by the broader system change' (Saltzman Chafetz 1990: 18). Against culturally determinist models of change, she questions the significance of shifts within gender ideologies and norms unless they are paralleled by transformations within the gender division of labour through which women increase their access to resource-generating work roles (1990: 41). The gender division of labour and the access it gives to material resources is a crucial determinant of levels of female emancipation or subordination. Indeed, in contrast to the prevailing focus in feminist theory on sexuality, she claims that although issues pertaining to sexual orientation are not irrelevant to gender system maintenance, compulsive and exclusive heterosexuality is not a fundamental bulwark of systemic reproduction. Lesbianism, in her view, is only harshly sanctioned when it is tied to social rebellion; it is against rebellion, not sexual preference *per se*, that societal repression is most strongly directed (1990: 90).

Whilst at points, Saltzman Chafetz seems to reassert a problematic base–superstructure distinction, her emphasis on the importance of relating intentional cultural shifts to unintentional systemic dynamics is vital if naive or one-sided accounts of transformation within gender norms are to be avoided. In the sense intended by Luhmann, there seems to be a autopoetic dimension to the reproduction of gender inequalities which the materialist insistence on the compulsory nature of the sex–gender system partially evokes: 'gender systems are highly resistant to substantial change toward [in]equality. Gender systems are structured so as to automatically reproduce themselves'

(1990: 94). The tendency, evident in much work on the discursive construction of the subject, to reduce gender to the question of sexual identity disregards these abstract, systemic and unintentional dynamics which may hinder or catalyse change. A further point highlighted by the materialist feminist insistence on an involuntary systemic aspect to change is that shifts within gender and other identity norms can be retrogressive as well as progressive, forms of stratification can increase as well as decrease. This tends to be overlooked in symbolic feminism and certain theories of detraditionalization where the implicit valorization of indeterminacy assumes that the breakdown of hegemonic norms is emancipatory *per se* (Adam 1996; Thompson 1996). In short, there is a need for a greater analytical distinction between changes in the form of gender inequality and progress; the decline of gender inequality along certain axes may trigger new forms of subordination in other areas (Walby 1990: 23).

Symbolic theories of gender differentiation provide a powerful understanding of the deep-seated nature of cultural categories and the levels of anxiety that their destabilization can provoke, but they do not explain sufficiently structural or institutional dimensions of domination. Material structures of domination are not reducible to symbolic patterns of gender differentiation, as Iris Young puts it: 'to regard male domination as identical with or derivable from gender differentiation . . . is to overpsychologize the social phenomena of male domination' (Young 1997: 27). Analogously, the tendency in certain types of feminist theory to produce an oversexualized account of gender may explain the discursive inculcation of predispositions to power but says little about the logic of material relations of power. The necessity of situating symbolic within material relations need not involve an assertion of the determining priority of the latter over the former, of base over superstructure. Rather it underlines the importance of distinguishing the respective internal logics of different sets of power relations and theorizing their interconnections in order to understand the complex and discontinuous ways in which individuals are disempowered. For example, certain types of male domination are not predicated on the prevention of women

and other marginal groups from acting but rather on the sys-
tematic transferral of the benefits of their contributions to
men (Young 1997: 32). This is not to deny the force of symbolic forms of disempowerment but it is to recognize that
the relation between symbolic codes of gender and concrete
practices is not isomorphic. This has long been recognized by
social anthropologists who note that meaning does not reside
in symbols but 'must be invested in and interpreted from
symbols by acting social beings' (Moore 1994: 74). In her work
on the construction of gender in Hagen culture, for example,
Marilyn Strathern points out that metaphorized notions of
masculinity and femininity are powerful because they are, to
some degree, free-floating and are not reflected in a straightforward fashion in the practices of men and women: 'gender
comprises a language in itself which furnishes idioms for refer-
ring to other qualities and relationships' (Strathern 1978: 173).
Not only are metaphors of masculinity and femininity used to
symbolize other social relations (of achievement, strength etc.),
but the symbolic representation of other social relations can
effect the use of gender metaphors in complex and often paradoxical ways. In sum, there is no necessary correlation between the existence of highly normative symbolic codes and
constricted individual practices. Nor, conversely, does it follow
that the loosening of gender norms need necessarily result in
an attenuation of other material inequalities. The phallocentric
drive to power does not provide an explanation of the many
ways in which gender inequalities are reproduced and maintained throughout the social structure. In short, complex
relations of autonomy and dependence are emerging in the
restructuring of gender relations that elude symbolic accounts
of subjectification and the absolutized models of change upon
which they are predicated.

While materialist analyses explain the deep-rooted nature of
gender inequalities and the uneven effects of their restructuring, it is important not to fall, on the other side, into a form of
material reductionism. Although recent materialist feminists
try to avoid overstated accounts of patriarchal domination,
determinist tendencies often re-enter their work, on a covert
level, because of the failure to develop mediatory categories of

the subject and agency. Such categories go some way to explaining the interconnections between different regimes of gender. This oversight is partly the result of a resistance on the part of materialist feminists to the tendency within symbolic feminism to filter all issues of gender relations through the lens of identity. While symbolic feminisms do not offer a sufficient account of the material dimensions of agency, they nonetheless draw attention to modalities of subjectivity and self-formation that materialist analysis overlooks. Highlighting processes of self-formation draws attention to an active, interpretative dynamic in agency without which an understanding of change would be rendered one-dimensional. For example, in *Having None of It*, Suzanne Francks documents a growing discrepancy between young women's expectations of social equality and the persistence of discriminatory practices and inequalities at work and in the domestic sphere. Although, on one level, such a disjunction endorses a materialist insistence on the necessity of placing an analysis of identity within the context of other relations of power, it also underscores the importance of a hermeneutic or interpretative perspective on change in order to examine the links between attitudinal shifts and structural transformation. Although there might not be a direct causal relation, attitudinal changes may contribute to a crescive alteration in shared social practices which, in turn, may have a transformatory impact on systemic tendencies in the manner of the so-called new social movements. In this respect, change is not the result of 'the vague tendency of the system, nor the undefined drive of change-oriented collectivities . . . but [of] the everyday conduct of common people, often quite far removed from any reformist intentions that are found to shape and reshape human societies' (Sztompka 1994: 39). The materialist emphasis on objective structures of inequality to the exclusion of a theory of agency may not detect the significant impact that such attitudinal shifts may have upon processes of social transformation. An act that may seem conformist, from a structural perspective, may in fact entail either a non-propositional content or high levels of self-consciousness, both of which may be indicative of slow but far-reaching cultural shifts. For example, the non-propositional content of agency can contribute to a transformation in social relations where experience which was not previously understandable becomes understandable. Psychoanalytic and constructionist accounts of subjectification both draw attention to this in terms of the often unrecognized effects of unconscious attachments and inculcated norms upon behaviour and self-understanding. However, because of the paucity of the account of agency offered in the negative paradigm, the ways in which this non-propositional content connects to broader social changes remain underelaborated.

From passive to active subject

The claim that the relations between material and symbolic structures need to be more precisely analysed in order to understand agency and change within gender is not in itself original. Indeed, although formulated in diverse ways, it has been a major preoccupation of feminist analyses of gender relations. The claim of this book, however, is that the prevailing conceptions of subjectification and agency constructed around a negative dynamic are not sufficient for thinking through such connections between the material and the symbolic. The essential passivity of the subject underlying the negative para-digm results in an etiolated conception of agency which can-not explain how individuals may respond in an unanticipated or creative fashion to complex social relations. A generative theory of subjectification provides a more dynamic theory of agency through which to examine how social actors may adapt and respond in an active fashion to the uncertainties unleashed in an increasingly differentiated social order. The symbolic and material determinisms that operate in much feminist theory seem to preclude such a generative account of subject forma-tion and autonomous agency.

None of the work of the thinkers examined here is sufficient on its own to offer a reconfigured account of agency. How-ever, their diverse formulations of the theme of the creativity of action cover some of the main theoretical dimensions that ought to be encompassed in such an account. Both Bourdieu and Ricoeur develop a dialectical account of temporality to explain the emergence of agency from constraint in a way that is precluded in the temporally uni-directional explanations of the negative paradigm of subjectification. Ricoeur develops this dialectic to yield a hermeneutic understanding of an active, interpretative dimension to agency expressed in the construction of a coherent self-identity. This idea of active appropriation which lies at the heart of self-formation has implications for a theory of change. It suggests that the central role played by a coherent notion of self in making sense of the flux of existence may act as a brake on the transformation of social relations – especially intimate relations which are peculiarly amenable to narrative structure. The effects of the need to maintain a coherent sense of self are significantly underestimated in certain types of constructionist thought, whose emphasis on the dissolution and refashioning of identity tends to overlook the embedded aspects of subjectivity. As Stuart Hall puts it: 'identity is not fixed, but it's not nothing either' (1997: 33).

Bourdieu's elaboration of the praxeological implications of a temporal dialectic also explains how constraint is generative of agency. Unlike Ricoeur, his thought lacks a strong hermeneutic dimension and this, in part, underlies the criticism that the concepts of habitus and the field are simply sophisticated reformulations of a materialist determinism. The analysis of agency in terms of the couplet habitus–field serves, however, to emphasize the necessity of situating any theory of agency within the context of power relations if voluntarism is to be avoided. Although Ricoeur's idea of a critical hermeneutics explicitly eschews any idea of the authenticity of experience, his failure to break out of a textual model of action blocks a sustained analysis of the material and social relations which traverse it. Without such a contextualization, the idea of a creative substrate to action may border on a naive account of agency premised on the unmediated nature of practice. The force of Bourdieu's idea of the field is that it locates agency in the context of material and social forces but, in so far as it expresses a principle of differentiation, it replaces a uni-directional determinism with a generative and refractory logic. The concept of the field offers a way of examining change within gender relations beyond the dichotomies of the public and the private or the symbolic and the material. The symbolic codes of masculinity and femininity are reproduced according to the distinct material relations or logic of a given field. This, in turn, suggests that change within gender relations is relatively discontinuous and uneven, although not completely fragmented, given the transferable nature of certain types of power relations across fields. Against oversimplified theories of detraditionalization, this idea also suggests that reflexive agency is not a universal feature of 'post-conventional' societies, but an unevenly emerging phenomenon dependent on a distinct configuration of power relations.

Whereas the work of Bourdieu and Ricoeur incorporates a fuller understanding of certain material and interpretative dynamics into a constructionist theory of subjectification, it is in the work of Castoriadis that the underpinnings of agency in the psyche are most fully explored. A psychoanalytical account of subjectification explains the deep-seated and often opaque investments which underlie action and which are particularly central to any analysis of how individuals relate to hegemonic gender norms. The force of Castoriadis's work is that the reconfiguration of the relation between psyche and society in terms of a relation of inherence opens up a psychoanalytical account of subjectification to a fuller understanding of the historicity of social structures. Although the ontological grounds of agency lie in the disjunction between psyche and social structure, the historically determinate nature of action is not effaced by being reduced to this self-identical principle of disjunction, as it is, for example, in ideas of agency as melancholia. By replacing univocal conceptions of the symbolic as the realm of instituted meaning with the more open idea of the social imaginary as the realm of the instituting–instituted, both the socially specific and creative aspects of agency can be more easily understood. At the most general level, Castoriadis's thought contributes towards understanding types of change which are not fully addressed in the negative paradigm because of its determinist tendencies. In certain respects, the exponentially rapid transformation of women's social status in industrialized societies is indicative of the underdetermined nature of social action and its inherent creativity.

The generative understanding of subjectification proposed here is not meant as a replacement but rather as a supplement to what has been characterized as the negative paradigm. The negative paradigm exemplified in the work of Foucault and Lacan offers a powerful explanation of the profound inscription of gender norms in the process of subject formation. However, the emphasis it places on the moment of subjection forecloses a more active and nuanced account of agency. Such a theory of agency is necessary to explain some of the ways women and men negotiate the problems and uncertainties that are a consequence of the restructuring of gender relations in late-capitalist societies.

NOTES

Chapter 2 Body, Position, Power

1 It is the extent to which Foucault draws attention to the constructed, socially contingent and hence mutable elements of identity that makes his work a central source for much recent thought.
Foucault's work on discipline shows how the body is not a natural
entity but is socially produced through regimes of knowledge and
power (*dispositif*). His later work shifts focus from 'technologies of
domination' to 'technologies of the self' and claims that identity is
not simply imposed from above, but is also actively determined
by individuals through the deployment of 'practices' of the self.
When this process of self-stylization becomes conscious, then the
potential for a reflexive or ethical form of self-fashioning – an
'aesthetics of existence' – emerges (Foucault 1985). Self-stylization
is an example of what Foucault calls the practice of liberty.

Despite its impact upon subsequent thought on the issue of
subjectification, there are certain difficulties in Foucault's thinking
of the nature of embodied identity which stem from his failure to
integrate fully the insights from his work on biopower with his
subsequent thought on practices of the self. This results in an
unresolved vacillation between determinism, on the one hand, and
voluntarism, on the other. From 'Nietzsche, Genealogy, History'
through to the first volume of *The History of Sexuality*, it is the
docile body which is inexorably worked upon by differing disciplinary regimes. The idea of discipline replaces dichotomized
understandings of corporeal repression and liberation – evident in
Marcuse's work, for example – with a more complex notion of

networks of control that are simultaneously constitutive of pleasure. The very means through which individuals are controlled also
provides the foundation for autonomous action. In other words,
resistance emerges from within the social and not from some
extra-social or unconscious source (Foucault 1980: 142). This
insight into the capacity of dominatory relations to fold back upon
themselves creating spaces of autonomy is undercut by Foucault's
failure to think through the materiality of the body. There is a tendency to conceive of the body as essentially a passive, blank surface
upon which power relations are inscribed. As a result, a form of uni-
directional determinism emerges which leads to an understanding
of the acquistion of gender identity as a relatively straightforward
and one-sided process of inculcation and normalization (McNay
1994: 100–4).

The tendency to an overdeterminism that marks Foucault's
work on discipline arises in part because the process of corporeal
construction is considered in isolation from a notion of agency.
Subjectivity tends to be regarded as an effect or 'present correlative'
of regimes of disciplinary control over the body (Foucault 1977:
29). This lack of a more substantive theory of agency undermines
the idea of resistance because there is no category of the active subject through which it may be realized. Foucault's work on practices
of the self corrects this imbalance by showing how the process
of subjectification involves not only bodily subjection, but also a
relatively autonomous form of self-construction (Foucault 1982).
However, although the concept of the 'docile body' is replaced with
the more productive notion of the 'reflexive' subject, the materiality
of the body remains unthought in so far as it is conceived as the
non-problematic backdrop to practices of the self. The impression
is given that corporeal identity, particularly sexual identity, is fully
amenable to a process of self-stylization. This failure to consider
fully the recalcitrance, resistances or failures that embodied being
may present to processes of self-fashioning manifests itself, for
example, in the emphasis on aesthetics of the self as a form of
ascesis or self-mastery which fails to consider the exclusionary
implications of such a masculine model of self-control for female
subjects (McNay 1992). More generally, the ways in which the
pre-conscious and unknowable elements of incorporated experience – suggested, for example, in the different psychoanalytic formulations of the imaginary and unconscious realms – might block
an ethics of the self are not taken into account (e.g. Grosz 1994a:
193–4).

This neglect to distinguish more precisely between aspects of subjectivity that are relatively amenable to self-fashioning and those that are more ineluctable arises partly from Foucault's rejection of the psychoanalytic concept of repression and associated notions of the unconscious, drives and desires. Foucault's reformulation of power as emerging within productive social relations, rather than as a repressive, psychic energy, undoubtedly has much force but it leaves him, in a sense, with a flattened-out view of the subject where the question of how it is possible to refashion more deeply inscribed elements of the self – such as sexual desire – is not adequately addressed. In so far as it underestimates the embodied aspects of existence, Foucault's final work bears traces of an abstract voluntarism which reformulates rather than breaks from a philosophy of consciousness.

2 Bourdieu defines praxeology as 'a universal anthropology which takes into account the historicity, and thus the relativity, of cognitive structures, while recording the fact that agents universally put to work such historical structures' (1992: 139).

3 In the light of this criticism, it is somewhat ironic that the idea of the performative has been criticized for being too voluntarist, a charge that Butler has convincingly refuted (Butler 1994: 33).

4 Butler herself acknowledges this in a recent article in *New Left Review* (Butler 1998).

5 It is also a problem in the work of social theorists such as Habermas who, by placing familial relations within the communicative sphere of the lifeworld, underestimates the extent to which they are crossed by an instrumental rationality that is regarded as pertaining to systems only (Fraser 1987; Dean 1996).

Chapter 3 Gender and Narrative

1 See special issue on narrative of *Critical Inquiry* (autumn 1980), 7/1.

2 Although he rejects a positivist method, Habermas also regards narrative as secondary to the communicative structures underlying social action. Narrative pertains to a postmodern generalization of aesthetic categories whose relativist implications undermine the possibility of emancipatory social critique (McCarthy 1987: xiii).

3 Attempts to express the lived experience of time in narrative result in the multiplication of aporias. There are three particular aporia that the narrative form reveals. First, the aporia resulting from the 'mutual occultation of phenomenological and cosmological

time', that is, the incompatibility between being in time and the lived experience of time. Second, the aporia between totality and temporalization expressed in the disjunction between the three 'ecstases' of time: future, past and present. Narrative tries to totalize this relation through such devices as causality and closure, but, in Ricoeur's view, there is always an uneasy tension between the 'horizon of expectation, retrieval of past heritages and occurrence of untimely present' (Ricoeur 1998: 250). This tension is manifest, for example, in the utopian imagination which places future expectations in a critical relation with the present. Utopia introduces alterity into the present which unsettles the seeming certainty of the latter. Finally, there is the aporia of the 'inscrutability of time' and the limits of narrative. This refers to the way in which the ultimate unknowability of time pushes narrative to its limit.

4 There is an ambiguity in Ricoeur about whether the idea of narrative should be properly understood as an ontological or quasi-ontological category (see Kerby 1991).

5 Central to the construction of narrative self-identity is a threefold process of understanding and appropriation defined as pre-understanding, configuration and refiguration. Mimesis$_1$ refers to the way in which a meaningful act of narration or emplotment is dependent upon a pre-understanding of the world of action and its meaningful structures: 'to imitate or represent action is first to preunderstand what human acting is, in its semantics, its symbolic system, its temporality' (Ricoeur 1983: 64). There are three dimensions to this pre-understanding: a structural dimension of understanding which denotes the ability to distinguish meaningful human action from physical movement or unreflexive behaviour; an understanding of the symbolic nature of human action; a pre-understanding of the temporal aspects of human action.

From the pre-understanding of the world of action emerges the second level of mimesis (mimesis$_2$) which involves the dynamic character of the configuring operation of narrative. Narrative and its chief strategy of emplotment does not involve the passive imitation of action, but rather its active mediation. The dynamic element lies in what Ricoeur calls the 'grasping together' that is constitutive of the configurational act in which narrative imposes order upon the heterogeneous fabric of events: 'it [narrative] draws from this manifold of events the unity of one temporal whole' (1983: 66). The configurational arrangement transforms the succession of events into one meaningful whole which is the correlate of the act of assembling the events together and makes the story followable. It imposes a sense of an ending and may establish an alternative sense of temporality in that the repetition of a story, governed as a whole by its way of ending, constitutes an alternative to the representation of time as flowing from the past toward the future (1983: 67). The construing of narrative in terms of this dynamic act of configuration reveals how mimesis is not simply an act of the imitative reproductive imagination but of the productive imagination (1983: 68).

The final level of mimesis (mimesis$_3$) involves the intersection of the world of the text and the world of the reader or, 'the intersection ... of the world configured by the poem and the world wherein real action occurs and unfolds its specific temporality' (1983: 71). Whilst narrative structure overdetermines the encounter between text and reader, the act of reading actualizes its capacity to be followed. This blurring of the inside–outside boundaries of the text, or fusion of horizons, rests upon the double or split referentiality of the text. This idea derives from Ricoeur's work on metaphor where he argues that if the sentence is taken as the basic unit of discourse, it is possible to see how language refers beyond itself: 'language is for itself the order of the Same. The world is its Other. The attestation of this otherness arises from language's reflexivity with regard to itself, whereby it knows itself as being *in* being in order to bear *on* being' (1983: 78). This idea of 'ontological attestation' runs contrary to structuralist accounts which reduce meaning to direct referentiality implied in the correlation between signifier and signified. The force of metaphor, for example, resides not in its direct referentiality, but in the degree to which it creates new meanings or projects a potential, alternative horizon, through its refiguration of the world: 'Metaphorical reference ... consists in the fact that the effacement of descriptive reference ... is revealed to be ... the negative condition for freeing a more radical power of reference to those aspects of our being-in-the-world that cannot be talked about directly' (1983: 80). Narrative is also metaphorical in that it projects a world in front of itself through its refiguration of the world in its temporal dimension.

Chapter 4 Psyche and Society

1 Lacan introduces the mediatory category of the symbolic into Freud's formulation of Oedipus which has been criticized for containing only a pre-Oedipal imaginary register and a post-Oedipal real (Wright 1992: 294).

Briefly, Lacan's basic argument is that sexual identity is achieved only at a cost to the individual as living being and that cost is related to the containment of the infant's bisexual nature within the dualism of heterosexuality. Entry into the symbolic realm of language breaks up the mother–child dyad and also terminates the infant's fantasies of complete union with the mother. This third term that breaks up the imaginary unity of the mother and child is associated with the 'law of the father', which leads to the claim of the phallocentric nature of the symbolic realm. This is to say that entry into the symbolic realm involves taking a place in relation to the phallus, i.e. 'symbolic castration'.

2 The phallus is the sign of this moment of primal repression or division within the subject which is simultaneously constitutive of sexual identity and of desire. Symbolic castration marks the formation and splitting of Desire. Desire is constituted in the symbolic realm in so far as it can be articulated only in speech and language. The act of articulating desire is indicative of identity in that it confers upon the subject a distinct or separate place, but this is only achieved at the cost of alienation. This is because it is possible to express demands in speech, but it is impossible to express all that underlies this demand. Desire then is constituted in this residue or gap between the articulated demand and that which underlies the demand. Thus desire is born at the moment of primal repression (*Urverdrängung*) between unconscious desire (to be reunited with the mother) and consciously expressed demand. This notion of the gap or residue leads to Lacan's understanding of desire as that which always exceeds or slips away in language, as that which cannot ever be fulfilled (Lacan 1982: 80).

3 In *Volatile Bodies*, Elizabeth Grosz also explores the inherence of pysche and society using the image of the Möbius strip which replaces dualistic understandings of the relation between psychical interior and corporeal exterior (mind–body, inside–outside) with the idea of torsion of one into another. Grosz claims that psychoanalysis yields a non-oppositional conception of mind and body in the idea of 'body image' which suggests a necessary interconstituency and relation of mutual determination between the biological and psycho-social domains. From the idea of mutual inherence emerges a concept of the body as a transitional entity in that corporeal identity is regarded as unfinished and as amenable to immense transformations. The implied causal primacy of the psyche is then reversed through a rereading of Nietzsche, Foucault, Deleuze

and Lingis where Grosz considers how the social inscription of the surface of the body generates psychical interiority. The Deleuzian idea of the 'body without organs' is suggestive of a denaturalized, univocal concept of being. The body without organs is a field of immanence of desire which resists transcendence and defies hierarchization. As a volatile entity, it is the site of a multiplicity of micro-struggles between competing power regimes.

4 This discontinuity is illustrated in the work of Sarah Koffman, who shows how the complaint amongst Freud's female patients that their mothers did not give them enough milk did not actually correspond to reality. Rather it involved the projection of feelings of frustration arising from the structurally inaccessible nature of desire onto the finite, external figure of the mother/wet-nurse. Whilst demonstrating that there is no one-to-one correspondence between fantasy and reality, Brennan argues that Koffman's work also illustrates that fantasies inevitably involve a process of projection into social reality: 'psychoanalysis is a theory of the derivation of certain fantasies and (inescapably) a theory of how fantasies go *out*, over there. Into the social, onto people and things who are thereby credited or confused with, or constructed by imaginary attributes' (Brennan 1990: 131).

5 The constitution of an object as desirable cannot be explained through reference to the characteristics of the missing object itself. Although the psyche has an irreducible relation to biological-corporeal reality, it is not one of simple determination. The oral drive may be inconceivable without the mouth but the mouth itself says little about the oral instinct in general and the significance it may acquire for an individual or within a given culture. Thus psychical working out is neither dictated by biology nor absolutely free with respect to it. Castoriadis uses the Freudian term of *anaclisis* (leaning on) to describe this relation of mutual inherence between the psyche and biological-corporeal reality. The notion of *anaclisis* cannot be accounted for within the traditional schemata of determinacy. Although the privileged somatic data will be taken up by the psyche, the manner in which it will be invested cannot be explained according to any causal schema: 'psychical working out will have to "take them into account" [somatic data], they will leave their mark on it – but which mark and in what manner cannot be reflected in the identitary frame of reference of determinacy' (Castoriadis 1987: 290).

6 Castoriadis uses the term inherence to typify not just the relation between the radical and social imaginaries but also the relation

between the somatic and the psyche and the natural and the social. See n. 5 above.

7 Language is central to Lacan's account of the formation of identity, yet the concept of language with which he works seems to be riven by an aporetic tension which mirrors the aporia in his conception of the symbolic discussed above. On the one hand, the fundamental instability of language arising from its negative, relational nature provides the idea of the impossibility of attaining fixed meaning and identity within the symbolic system. Yet, on the other hand, this instability is foreclosed with the imposition of the law of the father which installs an invariant phallocentric structure of meaning. The passage from the essential instability of language to its foreclosure by the domination of the phallocentric matrix is abrupt and renders the symbolic an incontestable structure.

8 In this sense, Castoriadis's understanding of alienation differs from that of Marx in that it is not class-specific. Although there is a class element to alienation in that it is connected to the power of one social class over the whole, there is also alienation irrespective of class connected to the institution of society. Once an institution is established and acquires its own materiality, it may appear to be autonomous by virtue of its possessing its own inertia and its own logic. Rather than recognizing itself as the source of these institutions, society becomes in thrall to these autonomized institutions. In Castoriadis's words: 'Alienation appears first of all as the alienation of a society to its institutions' (1987: 115).

REFERENCES

Adam, Barbara (1995). *Timewatch: The Social Analysis of Time*. Cambridge: Polity Press.

Adam, Barbara (1996). 'Detraditionalization and the Certainty of Uncertain Futures', in P. Heelas et al. (eds), *Detraditionalization: Critical Reflections on Authority and Identity*. Oxford: Basil Blackwell.

Adams, Parveen (1982). 'Family Affairs', *m/f*, 7: 3–14.

Adams, Parveen (1990). 'A Note on the Distinction between Sexual Division and Sexual Differences', in P. Adams and E. Cowie (eds), *The Woman in Question*. London: Verso.

Anderson, Pamela (1993). 'Having it Both Ways: Ricoeur's Hermeneutics of the Self', *Oxford Literary Review*, 15: 227–52.

Alexander, Jeremy (1994). *Fin de Siècle Social Theory: Relativism, Reduction and the Problem of Reason*. London: Verso.

Bailey, Lucy (1999). 'Birth Rites: Power, the Body and the Self in the Transition to Motherhood', PhD thesis, University of Bristol.

Barbre, Joy Webster and Personal Narratives Group (eds) (1989). *Interpreting Women's Lives: Feminist Theory and Personal Narratives*. Indiana: Indiana University Press.

Barthes, Roland (1982). 'Introduction to the Structural Analysis of Narrative', in S. Sontag (ed.), *Barthes: Selected Writings*. London: Fontana.

Bartky, S. (1988). 'Foucault, Femininity and the Modernization of Patriarchal Power', in I. Diamond and L. Quinby (eds), *Feminism and Foucault: Reflections on Resistance*. Boston: Northeastern University Press.

Baudrillard, Jean (1983). *Simulations*. New York: Semiotext(e).

Bauman, Zygmunt (1991). *Modernity and Ambivalence*. Cambridge: Polity Press.

Bauman, Zygmunt (1995). *Life in Fragments: Essays in Postmodern Morality*. Oxford: Blackwell Publishers.

Beauvoir, Simone de (1972). *The Second Sex*. Harmondsworth: Penguin.

Beck, Ulrich (1992). *Risk Society: Towards a New Modernity*. London: Sage.

Beck, Ulrich and Beck-Gernsheim, Elisabeth (1995). *The Normal Chaos of Love*. Cambridge: Polity Press.

Bell, David et al. (1994). 'All Hyped Up and No Place to Go', *Gender, Place and Culture: A Journal of Feminist Geography*, 1 (1): 31–47.

Bell, Vikki (ed.) (1999). *Performativity and Belonging*. Special issue of *Theory, Culture and Society*, 16.

Benhabib, Selya (1986). *Critique, Norm and Utopia: A Study of the Foundations of Critical Theory*. New York: Columbia University Press.

Benhabib, Selya (1992). *Situating the Self: Gender, Community and Postmodernism in Contemporary Ethics*. Cambridge: Polity Press.

Benhabib, Selya (1995). 'Subjectivity, Historiography and Politics', in S. Benhabib et al. (eds), *Feminist Contentions: A Philosophical Exchange*. London: Routledge.

Benhabib, Selya and Dallmayr, Fred (eds) (1991). *The Communicative Ethics Controversy*. London: MIT Press.

Benjamin, Jessica (1978). 'Authority and the Family Revisited: or, a World without Fathers', *New German Critique*, 13: 35–57.

Benjamin, Jessica (1982). 'Shame and Sexual Politics', *New German Critique*, 27: 151–9.

Bhabha, Homi K. (1983). 'Difference, Discrimination and the Discourse of Colonialism', in F. Barker et al. (eds), *The Politics of Theory* (Colchester: University of Essex).

Bhabha, Homi (1994). *The Location of Culture*. London: Routledge.

Bourdieu, Pierre (1977). *Outline of a Theory of Practice*. Cambridge: Cambridge University Press.

Bourdieu, Pierre (1979). *Distinction: A Social Critique of the Judgement of Taste*. London: Routledge and Kegan Paul.

Bourdieu, Pierre (1989). *La noblesse d'Etat: grandes écoles et esprit de corps*. Paris: Editions de Minuit. Eng. tr. *The State Nobility: Elite Schools in the Field of Power* (1998), Cambridge: Polity Press.

Bourdieu, Pierre (1990a). *The Logic of Practice*. Cambridge: Polity Press.

Bourdieu, Pierre (1990b). 'La domination masculine', *Actes de la Recherche en Sciences Sociales*, 84 (Sept.): 2–31.

Bourdieu, Pierre (1990c). *In Other Words: Essay Towards a Reflexive Sociology*. Cambridge: Polity Press.

Bourdieu, Pierre (1991). *Language and Symbolic Power*. Cambridge: Polity Press.

Bourdieu, Pierre (1992). *An Invitation to Reflexive Sociology*. Cambridge: Polity Press.

Bourdieu, Pierre (1993). *Sociology in Question*. London: Sage.

Bourdieu, Pierre (1996). 'On the Family as a Realized Category', *Theory, Culture and Society*, 13 (3): 19–26.

Bourdieu, Pierre (1999). *La domination masculine*. Paris: Editions du Seuil.

Bourdieu, Pierre and Eagleton, Terry (1992). 'Doxa and Common Life', *New Left Review*, 191 (Jan.–Feb.): 111–21.

Bourdieu, Pierre and Passeron, Jean-Claude (1977). *Reproduction in Education, Society and Culture*. London: Sage.

Braidotti, Rosi (1989). 'The Politics of Ontological Difference', in T. Brennan (ed.), *Between Feminism and Psychoanalysis*. London: Routledge.

Braidotti, Rosi (1994). *Nomadic Subjects: Embodiment and Sexual Difference in Contemporary Feminist Theory*. New York: Columbia University Press.

Brennan, Teresa (ed.) (1989). *Between Feminism and Psychoanalysis*. London: Routledge.

Brennan, Teresa (1990). 'An Impasse in Psychoanalysis and Feminism', in S. Gunew (ed.), *A Reader in Feminist Knowledge*. London: Routledge.

Brennan, Teresa (1993). *History after Lacan*. London: Routledge.

Brison, Susan (1997). 'Outliving Oneself: Trauma, Memory and Personal Identity', in D. Meyers (ed.), *Feminist Rethink the Self*. Oxford: Westview Press.

Bruner, Jerome (1987). 'Life as Narrative'. *Social Research*, 54: 11–32.

Butler, Judith (1987). 'Variations on Sex and Gender: Beauvoir, Wittig and Foucault', in S. Benhabib and D. Cornell (eds), *Feminism as Critique: Essays on the Politics of Gender in Late-Capitalist Societies*. Cambridge: Polity Press.

Butler, Judith (1990). *Gender Trouble: Feminism and the Subversion of Identity*. London: Routledge.

Butler Judith (1992). 'Contingent Foundations: Feminism and the Question of "Postmodernism"', in Judith Butler and Joan W. Scott (eds), *Feminists Theorize the Political*. London: Routledge.

Butler, Judith (1993a). *Bodies that Matter: On the Discursive Limits of Sex*. London: Routledge.

Butler, Judith (1993b). 'Critically Queer', *GLQ: A Journal of Lesbian and Gay Studies*, 1: 17–32.

Butler, Judith (1994). 'Gender as Performance: An Interview with Judith Butler', *Radical Philosophy*, 67: 32–9.

Butler, Judith (1997a). *Excitable Speech: A Politics of the Performative.* London: Routledge.

Butler, Judith (1997b). *The Psychic Life of Power: Theories in Subjection.* Stanford, Calif: Stanford University Press.

Butler, Judith (1998). 'Marxism and the Merely Cultural', *New Left Review*, 227: 33–44.

Calhoun, Craig (1983). 'Habitus, Field and Capital: The Question of Historical Specificity', in C. Calhoun, E. LiPuma and M. Postone (eds), *Bourdieu: Critical Perspectives.* Cambridge: Polity Press.

Campbell, Colin (1996). 'Detraditionalization, Character and the Limits to Agency', in P. Heelas et al. (eds), *Detraditionalization: Critical Reflections on Authority and Identity.* Oxford: Blackwell Publishers.

Cancian, Francesca (1989). 'Gender and Power: Love and Power in the Public and Private Spheres', in A. S. Solnick and J. H. Solnick (eds), *Family in Transition: Rethinking Marriage, Sexuality, Child Rearing and Family Organization.* London: Scott Foresman.

Carr, David (1985). 'Life and the Narrator's Art', in H. J. Silverman and D. Idhe (eds), *Hermeneutics and Deconstruction.* Albany: State University of New York Press.

Castoriadis, Cornelius (1984). *Crossroads in the Labyrinth.* Brighton: Harvester.

Castoriadis, Cornelius (1987). *The Imaginary Institution of Society.* Cambridge: Polity Press.

Castoriadis, Cornelius (1991). *Philosophy, Politics and Autonomy: Essays in Political Philosophy.* Oxford: Oxford University Press.

Connell, Robert W. (1987). *Gender and Power: Society, the Person and Sexual Politics.* Cambridge: Polity Press.

Connell, Robert W. (1995). *Masculinities.* Cambridge: Polity Press.

Coole, Diana (1996). 'Habermas and the Question of Alterity', in M. Passerin D'Entrèves and S. Benhabib (eds), *Habermas and the Unfinished Project of Modernity: Critical Essays on the Philosophical Discourse of Modernity.* Cambridge: Polity Press.

Cornell, Drucilla (1992). *The Philosophy of the Limit.* London: Routledge.

Cornell, Drucilla (1993). *Transformations: Recollective Imagination and Sexual Difference.* London: Routledge.

Cornell, Drucilla (1995). 'What is Ethical Feminism?', in S. Benhabib et al. (eds), *Feminist Contentions: A Philosophical Exchange.* London: Routledge.

Cornell, Drucilla and Thurschwell, Adam (1987). 'Feminism, Negativity, Intersubjectivity', in S. Benhabib and D. Cornell (eds), *Feminism as Critique: Essays on the Politics of Gender in Late-Capitalist Societies*. Cambridge: Polity Press.

Craib, Ian (1994). *The Importance of Disappointment*. London: Routledge.

Crespi, Franco (1989). *Social Action and Power*. Oxford: Basil Blackwell.

Crompton, Rosemary and Mann, Michael (eds) (1986). *Gender and Stratification*. Cambridge: Polity Press.

Davies, Karen (1990). *Women and Time: Weaving the Strands of Everyday Life*. Aldershot: Avebury.

Dean, Jodi (1996). *Solidarity of Strangers: Feminism after Identity Politics*. London: University of California Press.

De Lauretis, Teresa (1984). *Alice Doesn't: Feminism, Semiotics, Cinema*. London: Macmillan.

De Lauretis, Teresa (1987). *Technologies of Gender: Essays on Theory, Film and Fiction*. London: Macmillan.

D'Emilio, John (1984). 'Capitalism and Gay Identity', in A. Snitow et al. (eds), *Powers of Desire: The Politics of Sexuality*. London: Virago.

Dews, Peter (1995). *The Limits of Disenchantment: Essays on Contemporary European Philosophy*. London: Verso.

Diamond, Irene and Quinby, Lee (eds) (1988). *Feminism and Foucault: Reflections on Resistance*. Boston: Northeastern University Press.

Diprose, R. (1994). *The Bodies of Women: Ethics, Embodiment and Sexual Difference*. London: Routledge.

Dollimore, Jonathan (1991). *Sexual Dissidence: Augustine to Wilde, Freud to Foucault*. Oxford: Clarendon Press.

Duncombe, Jean and Marsden, Dennis (1993). 'Love and Intimacy: The Gender Division of Emotion and "Emotion Work"', *Sociology*, 27: 221–41.

Dubois, Ellen C., Dunlap, Mary C., Gilligan, Carol J., MacKinnon, Catherine A. and Menkel-Meadow, Carrie J. (1985). 'Feminist Discourse, Moral Values and the Law – A Conversation', *Buffalo Law Review*, 34: 11–87.

Elliott, Anthony (1992). *Social Theory and Psychoanalysis in Transition: Self and Society from Freud to Kristeva*. Oxford: Basil Blackwell.

Ermarth, Elizabeth D. (1989). 'The Solitude of Women and Social Time', in F. J. Forman and C. Sowton (eds), *Taking our Time: Feminist Perspectives on Temporality*. Oxford: Pergamon.

Etzioni, Amitai (1968). *Active Society*. New York: Free Press.

Fanon, Franz (1968). *Black Skin, White Masks*. London: MacGibbon and Kee.

Featherstone, Mike (1992). 'Postmodernism and the Aestheticization of Everyday Life', in S. Lash and J. Friedman (eds), *Modernity and Identity*. Oxford: Basil Blackwell.

Field, Nicola (1997). 'Identity and the Lifestyle Market', in R. Hennessy and C. Ingraham (eds), *Materialist Feminism: A Reader in Class, Difference and Women's Lives*. London: Routledge.

Fishman, Pamela (1978). 'Interaction: The Work Women Do', *Social Problems*, 25: 397–406.

Fiske, John (1989). *Understanding Popular Culture*. London: Unwin Hyman.

Flax, Jane (1993). *Disputed Subjects: Essays on Psychoanalysis, Politics and Philosophy*. London: Routledge.

Foucault, Michel (1977). *Discipline and Punish: The Birth of the Prison*. Harmondsworth: Peregrine.

Foucault, Michel (1978). *The History of Sexuality: An Introduction*. Harmondsworth: Penguin.

Foucault, Michel (1980). *Power/Knowledge: Selected Interviews and Other Writings*, ed. C. Gordon. Brighton: Harvester.

Foucault, Michel (1982). 'The Subject and Power', in H. Dreyfus and P. Rabinow, *Michel Foucault: Beyond Structuralism and Hermeneutics*. Chicago: Chicago University Press.

Foucault, Michel (1985). *The Use of Pleasure*. Harmondsworth: Penguin.

Foucault, Michel (1988). 'An Aesthetics of Existence', in L. Kritzman (ed.), *Politics, Philosophy, Culture: Interviews and Other Writings 1977–1984*. London: Routledge.

Franks, Suzanne (1999). *Having None of It: Women, Men and the Future of Work*. London: Granta Books.

Fraser, Nancy (1989). 'What's Critical about Critical Theory? The Case of Habermas and Gender', in *Unruly Practices: Power, Discourse and Gender in Contemporary Social Theory*. Cambridge: Polity Press.

Fraser, Nancy (1995). 'False Antitheses', 'Pragmatism, Feminism, and the Linguistic Turn', in S. Benhabib et al. (eds), *Feminist Contentions: A Philosophical Exchange*. London: Routledge.

Fraser, Nancy (1997). *Justice Interruptus: Critical Reflections on the 'Postsocialist' Condition*. London: Routledge.

Fraser, Nancy and Nicholson, Linda (1990). *Feminism/Postmodernism*. London: Routledge.

Fuss, Diana (1995). *Identification Papers*. London: Routledge.

Gallop, Jane (1982). *Feminism and Psychoanalysis: The Daughter's Seduction*. New York: Columbia University Press.

Garber, Marjorie (1992). *Vested Interests: Cross Dressing and Cultural Anxiety*. London: Routledge.

Garnham, Nicholas and Williams, Raymond (1980). 'Pierre Bourdieu and the Sociology of Culture: An Introduction', *Media, Culture and Society*, 2: 209–23.

Gasché, Rodolphe (1994). 'Yes Absolutely: Unlike Any Writing Pen', in E. Laclau (ed.), *The Making of Political Identities*. London: Verso.

Gatens, Moira (1991). *Feminism and Philosophy: Perspectives on Difference and Equality*. Cambridge: Polity Press.

German, Lindsey (1997). 'Theories of the Family', in R. Hennessy and C. Ingraham (eds), *Materialist Feminism: A Reader in Class, Difference and Women's Lives*. London: Routledge.

Giddens, Anthony (1992). *The Transformation of Intimacy: Sexuality, Love and Eroticism in Modern Societies*. Cambridge: Polity Press.

Gilmore, Leigh (1994). *Autobiographics: A Feminist Theory of Women's Self Representation*. London: Cornell University Press.

Ginsburg, Faye (1989). 'Dissonance and Harmony: The Symbolic Function of Abortion in Activists' Life Stories', in J. W. Barbre/Personal Narratives Group (eds), *Interpreting Women's Lives: Feminist Theory and Personal Narratives*. Indiana: Indiana University Press.

Godelier, Maurice (1984). *The Mental and the Material: Thought, Economy and Society*. London: Verso.

Grosz, Elizabeth (1990). *Jacques Lacan: A Feminist Introduction*. London: Routledge.

Grosz, Elizabeth (1994a). *Volatile Bodies: Towards a Corporeal Feminism*. Bloomington and Indianapolis: Indiana University Press.

Grosz, Elizabeth (1994b). 'Experimental Desire: Rethinking Queer Subjectivity', in J. Copjec (ed.), *Supposing the Subject*. London: Verso.

Habermas, Jürgen (1985). *The Philosophical Discourse of Modernity*. Cambridge: Polity Press.

Hall, Stuart (1996). 'What is this "Black" in Black Popular Culture?', in D. Morely and K. H. Chen (eds), *Stuart Hall: Critical Dialogues in Cultural Studies*. London: Routledge.

Hall, Stuart (1997). 'Interview on Culture and Power', *Radical Philosophy*, 86: 24–41.

Hartmann, Heidi (1981). 'The Unhappy Marriage of Marxism and Feminism: Towards a More Progressive Union', in L. Sargent (ed.), *Women and Revolution: A Discussion of the Unhappy Marriage of Marxism and Feminism*. London: Pluto Press.

Hekman, Susan (1995). 'Subjects and Agents: The Question for Feminism', in J. Kegan Gardiner (ed.), *Provoking Agents: Gender and Agency in Theory and Practice*. Chicago: University of Illinois Press.

Held, Victoria (1987). 'Feminism and Moral Theory', in E. Kittay and D. Meyers (eds), *Women and Moral Theory*. Totowa, NJ: Rowman and Littlefield.

Hennessy, Rosemary (1992). *Materialist Feminism and the Politics of Discourse*. London: Routledge.

Henriques, Julian et al. (1984). *Changing the Subject: Psychology, Social Regulation and Subjectivity*. London: Routledge.

Hill, Thomas (1987). 'The Importance of Autonomy', in E. Kittay and D. Meyers (eds), *Women and Moral Theory*. Totowa, NJ: Rowman and Littlefield.

Holloway, Wendy (1984). 'Gender Difference and the Production of Subjectivity', in J. Henriques et al. (eds), *Changing the Subject: Psychology, Social Regulation and Subjectivity*. London: Methuen.

Honig, Bonnie (1996). 'Difference, Dilemmas and the Politics of Home', in S. Benhabib (ed.), *Democracy and Difference: Contesting the Boundaries of the Political*. Princeton: Princeton University Press.

Howard, Dick (1988). *The Marxian Legacy*. London: Macmillan.

Hull, Carrie (1997). 'The Need in Thinking: Materiality in Theodor W. Adorno and Judith Butler', *Radical Philosophy*, 84: 22–33.

Jardine, Alice (1985). *Gynesis: Configurations of Woman and Modernity*. New York: Cornell University Press.

Joas, Hans (1996). *The Creativity of Action*. Cambridge: Polity Press.

Joas, Hans (1998). 'The Autonomy of the Self: The Meadian Heritage and its Postmodern Challenge', *European Journal of Social Theory*, 1: 7–18.

Johnson, Patricia (1988). 'Feminism and Images of Autonomy', *Radical Philosophy*, 50: 26–30.

Kaplan, E. Ann (1993). 'Madonna Politics: Perversion, Repression or Subversion? Or Masks and/as Mastery', in C. Schwichtenberg (ed.), *The Madonna Connection: Representational Politics, Subcultural Identities, and Cultural Theory*. Oxford: Westview Press.

Kearney, Richard (1991). *Poetics of Imagining: From Husserl to Lyotard*. London: HarperCollins Academic.

Kearney, Richard (ed.) (1996). *Paul Ricoeur: The Hermeneutics of Action*. London: Sage.

Kellner, Douglas (1992). 'Popular Culture and the Construction of Postmodern Identities', in S. Lash and J. Friedman (eds), *Modernity and Identity*. Oxford: Basil Blackwell.

Kerby, Anthony (1991). *Narrative and the Self*. Bloomington: Indiana University Press.

Kosselleck, Reinhart (1985). *Futures Past: On the Semantics of Historical Time*. Cambridge, Mass.: MIT Press.

Kristeva, Julia (1980). *Pouvoirs de l'horreur: Essai sur l'abjection*. Paris: Editions du Seuil.

Lacan, Jacques (1977a). 'The Mirror Stage as Formative of the Function of the I', in *Ecrits: A Selection*, trans. A. Sheridan. London: Routledge.

Lacan, Jacques (1977b). 'The Function and Field of Speech and Language in Psychoanalysis', in *Ecrits: A Selection*, trans. A. Sheridan. London: Routledge.

Lacan, Jacques (1977c). 'The Subject and Other: Alienation', in J. A. Miller (ed.), *The Four Fundamental Concepts of Psychoanalysis*. London: Hogarth Press.

Lacan, Jacques (1982). 'The Meaning of the Phallus', in J. Mitchell and J. Rose (eds), *Feminine Sexuality: Jacques Lacan and the Ecole Freudienne*. London: Macmillan.

Laclau, Ernesto (1994). *The Making of Political Identities*. London: Verso.

Laclau, Ernesto and Mouffe, Chantal (1985). *Hegemony and Socialist Strategy: Towards a Radical Democratic Politics*. London: Verso.

Laplanche, Jean and Pontalis, Jean-Bertrand (1973). *The Language of Psychoanalysis*. London: Hogarth Press.

Lara, Maria Pia (1998). *Moral Textures: Feminist Narratives in the Public Sphere*. Cambridge: Polity Press.

Lash, Scott (1990). *Sociology of Postmodernism*. London: Routledge.

Lefort, Claude (1986). *The Political Forms of Modern Society: Bureaucracy, Democracy, Totalitarianism*. Cambridge: Polity Press.

Leland, Dorothy (1992). 'Adequate Political Psychology', in N. Fraser and S. L. Bartky (eds), *Revaluing French Feminism: Critical Essays on Difference, Culture and Agency*. Indianapolis: Bloomington University Press.

Lloyd, Moya (1999). 'Performativity, Parody, Politics', *Theory, Culture and Society*, 16 (2): 195–213.

Lovibond, Sabina (1989). 'Feminism and Postmodernism', *New Left Review*, 178: 5–28.

Luhmann, Niklas (1986). *Love as Passion: The Codification of Intimacy*. Cambridge: Polity Press.

Luhmann, Niklas (1995). *Social Systems*. Stanford, Calif.: Stanford University Press.

Lyotard, Jean-François (1984). *The Postmodern Condition: A Report on Knowledge*. Manchester: Manchester University Press.

McCarthy, Thomas (1987). 'Introduction', in J. Habermas, *The Philosophical Discourse of Modernity*. Cambridge: Polity Press.

McCarthy, Thomas (1991). 'Complexity and Democracy: Or the Seducements of Systems Theory', in A. Honneth and H. Joas (eds),

Communicative Action: Essays on Jürgen Habermas's 'The Theory of Communicative Action'. Cambridge: Polity Press.

McClintock, Anne (1995). *Imperial Leather: Race, Gender and Sexuality in the Colonial Contest*. London: Routledge.

McNay, Lois (1992). *Foucault and Feminism: Power, Gender and the Self*. Cambridge: Polity Press.

McNay, Lois (1994). *Foucault: A Critical Introduction*. Cambridge: Polity Press.

McNay, Lois (1996). 'Michel de Certeau and the Ambivalent Everyday', *Social Semiotics*, 6 (1): 61–81.

McNay, Lois (1998). 'Foucault and Agonistic Democracy', in A. Carter and G. Stokes (eds), *Liberal Democracy and its Critics*. Cambridge: Polity Press.

McNay, Lois (1999). 'Gender, Habitus and the Field: Pierre Bourdieu and the Limits of Reflexivity', *Theory, Culture and Society*, 16.

Maffesoli, Michel (1988). *Les temps de tribus: le déclin de l'individualisme dans les sociétés de masse*. Paris: Méridiens Klincksieck.

Maffesoli, Michel (1996). *Ordinary Knowledge: An Introduction to Interpretative Sociology*. Cambridge: Polity Press.

Mann, Patricia (1994). *Micro-politics: Agency in a Postfeminist Era*. Minneapolis: University of Minnesota Press.

Meehan, Johanna (1995). *Feminists Read Habermas: Gendering the Subject of Discourse*. London: Routledge.

Mink, Louis O. (1970). 'History and Fiction as Modes of Comprehension', *New Literary History*, 1 (3): 542–58.

Mitchell, Juliet (1974). *Psychoanalysis and Feminism*. Harmondsworth: Penguin.

Mitchell, W. (1980). 'Editor's Note: On Narrative', *Critical Inquiry*, 7: 1–4.

Moore, Henrietta (1994). *A Passion for Difference: Essays in Anthropology and Gender*. Cambridge: Polity Press.

Norris, Christopher (1993). *The Truth about Postmodernism*. Oxford: Basil Blackwell.

O'Brien, P. (1982). *The Promise of Punishment: Prisons in Nineteenth Century France*. Princeton: Princeton University Press.

Offe, Claus (1987). 'New Social Movements', in C. Maier (ed.), *Changing Boundaries of the Political: Essays on the Evolving Balance between the State and Society, Public and Private in Europe*. Cambridge: Cambridge University Press.

Osborne, Peter and Segal, Lynne (1994). 'Gender as Performance: An Interview with Judith Butler', *Radical Philosophy*, 67: 32–9.

Pellegrini, Ann (1997). *Performance Anxieties: Staging Psychoanalysis, Staging Race*. London: Routledge.

Plaza, Monique (1978). 'Phallomorphic Power and the Psychology of Women', *Ideology and Consciousness*, 4: 4–36.

Plummer, Kenneth (1995). *Telling Sexual Stories: Power, Change and Social Worlds*. London: Routledge.

Polkinghorne, Donald (1988). *Narrative Knowing and the Human Sciences*. Albany: State University of New York Press.

Radway, Janice (1987). *Reading the Romance*. London: Verso.

Ragland-Sullivan, Ellie (1986). *Jacques Lacan and the Philosophy of Psychoanalysis*. Urbana: University of Illinois Press.

Ramazonoglu, Caroline (1993). *Up Against Foucault: Explorations of Some Tensions between Foucault and Feminism*. London: Routledge.

Richardson, Diane (1996). *Theorizing Heterosexuality: Telling it Straight*. Oxford: Oxford University Press.

Ricoeur, Paul (1974). 'Structure, Word, Event', in P. Ricoeur, *The Conflict of Interpretations*. Evanston, Ill.: Northwestern University Press.

Ricoeur, Paul (1981). *Hermeneutics and the Human Sciences: Essays on Language, Action and Interpretation*. Cambridge: Cambridge University Press.

Ricoeur, Paul (1983). *Time and Narrative, vol. 1*. Chicago: University of Chicago Press.

Ricoeur, Paul (1986). *Lectures on Ideology and Utopia*. New York: Columbia University Press.

Ricoeur, Paul (1988). *Time and Narrative, vol. 3*. Chicago: University of Chicago Press.

Ricoeur, Paul (1991a). *From Text to Action: Essays in Hermeneutics, II*. London: Northwestern University Press.

Ricoeur, Paul (1991b). 'Life: A Story in Search of a Narrator', in M. Valdes (ed.), *A Ricoeur Reader: Reflection and Imagination*. Hemel Hempstead: Harvester Wheatsheaf.

Ricoeur, Paul (1992). *Oneself as Another*. London: University of Chicago Press.

Ricoeur, Paul (1993). 'Self as Ipse', in B. Johnson (ed.), *Freedom and Interpretation: The Oxford Amnesty Lectures 1992*. London: Basic Books.

Ricoeur, Paul (1994). 'Imagination in Discourse and Action', in G. Robertson and J. Rundell (eds), *Rethinking Imagination*. London: Routledge.

Ricoeur, Paul (1998). *Critique and Conviction: Conversations with François Azouvi and Marc de Launay*. Cambridge: Polity Press.

Riley, Denise (1988). *'Am I that Name?' Feminism and the Category of Woman in History.* London: Macmillan.

Rose, Gillian (1984). *Dialectic of Nihilism: Poststructuralism and Law.* Oxford: Basil Blackwell.

Rose, Jacqueline (1982). 'Introduction – II', in J. Mitchell and J. Rose (eds), *Feminine Sexuality: Jacques Lacan and the École freudienne.* London: Macmillan.

Rose, Jacqueline (1986). *Sexuality in the Field of Vision.* London: Verso.

Rubin, Gayle (1975). 'The Traffic in Women: Notes on the "Political Economy" of Sex', in R. Reiter (ed.), *Toward an Anthropology of Women.* New York: Monthly Review Press.

Saltzman Chafetz, Janet (1990). *Gender Equity: An Integrated Theory of Stability and Change.* London: Sage.

Scott, Joan (1991). 'The Evidence of Experience', Critical Inquiry, 17: 773–97.

Sedgewick, Eve (1994). *Epistemology of the Closet.* Harmondsworth: Penguin.

Segal, Lynne (1990). *Slow Motion: Changing Masculinities, Changing Men.* London: Virago.

Sennett, Richard (1976). *The Fall of Public Man.* New York: Knopf.

Silverman, Kaja (1992). *Male Subjectivity at the Margins.* London: Routledge.

Smith, Dorothy (1987). *The Everyday as Problematic: A Feminist Sociology.* Milton Keynes: Open University Press.

Smith, Dorothy (1990). *The Conceptual Practices of Power: A Feminist Sociology of Knowledge.* Boston: Northeastern University Press.

Smith, Paul (1988). *Discerning the Subject.* Minneapolis: University of Minnesota Press.

Smith, Robert (1996). 'The Death Drive Does Not Think', *Common Knowledge*, 5 (1): 59–75.

Somers, Margaret R. and Gibson, Gloria D. (1994). 'Reclaiming the Epistemological "Other": Narrative and the Social Constitution of Identity', in C. Calhoun (ed.), *Social Theory and the Politics of Identity.* Oxford: Basil Blackwell.

Soper, Kate (1989). 'Feminism as Critique', *New Left Review*, 176: 91–114.

Soper, Kate (1990). 'Feminism, Humanism and Postmodernism', *Radical Philosophy*, 55: 11–17.

Spelman, Elizabeth (1990). *Inessential Woman: Problems of Exclusion in Feminist Thought.* London: Woman's Press.

Spivak, Gayatri (1993). *Outside in the Teaching Machine.* London: Routledge.

Stanley, Liz and Wise, Sue (eds) (1993). *Breaking Out Again: Feminist Ontology and Epistemology*. London: Macmillan.

Strathern, Marilyn (1978). 'The Achievement of Sex: Paradoxes in Hagen Gender-Thinking', in W. Schwimmer (ed.), *The Yearbook of Symbolic Anthropology*. London: Hurst.

Sztompka, Piotr (1994). *Agency and Structure: Reorienting Social Theory*. Reading: Gordon and Breach Science Publishers.

Thompson, John B. (1981). *Critical Hermeneutics: A Study in the Thought of Paul Ricoeur and Jürgen Habermas*. Cambridge: Cambridge University Press.

Thompson, John (1984). *Studies in the Theory of Ideology*. Cambridge: Polity Press.

Thompson, John (1996). 'Tradition and Self in a Mediated World', in P. Heelas et al. (eds), *Detraditionalization*. Oxford: Basil Blackwell.

Thompson, John and Held, David (eds) (1982). *Habermas: Critical Debates*. London: Macmillan.

Touraine, Alain (1977). *The Voice and the Eye: An Analysis of Social Movements*. Cambridge: Cambridge University Press.

Turner, Bryan (1991). 'Recent Developments in the Theory of the Body', in M. Featherstone et al. (eds), *The Body: Social Process and Cultural Theory*. London: Sage.

Ussher, Jane (1997). *Fantasies of Femininity: Reframing the Boundaries of Sex*. London: Penguin.

VanEvery, Jo (1995). *Heterosexual Women Changing the Family*. London: Taylor and Francis.

Violi, Patrizia (1992). 'Gender, Subjectivity and Language', in G. Bock and S. James (eds), *Beyond Equality and Difference: Citizenship, Feminist Politics and Female Subjectivity*. London, Routledge.

Walby, Sylvia (1990). *Theorizing Patriarchy*. Oxford: Basil Blackwell.

Walby, Sylvia (1992). 'Post-Post-Modernism? Theorizing Social Complexity', in M. Barrett and A. Phillips (eds), *Destabilizing Theory: Contemporary Feminist Debates*. Cambridge: Polity Press.

Walby, Sylvia (1997). *Gender Transformations*. London: Routledge.

Weir, Allison (1995). 'Toward a Model of Self-Identity: Habermas and Kristeva', in J. Meehan (ed.), *Feminists Read Habermas: Gendering the Subject of Discourse*. London: Routledge.

Weir, Allison (1996). *Sacrificial Logics: Feminist Theory and the Critique of Identity*. London: Routledge.

Whitebook, Joel (1995). *Perversion and Utopia: A Study in Psychoanalysis and Critical Theory*. London: MIT Press.

Whitebook, Joel (1996). 'Intersubjectivity and the Monadic Core of the Psyche: Habermas and Castoriadis on the Unconscious', in

M. Passerin d'Entrèves and S. Benhabib (eds), *Habermas and the Unfinished Project of Modernity: Critical Essays on the Philosophical Discourse of Modernity*. Cambridge: Polity Press.

Willis, Ellen (1988). 'Comment', in L. Grossberg and C. Nelson (eds), *Marxism and the Interpretation of Culture*. London: Macmillan.

Winship, Janice (1985). 'A Girl Needs to get "Street-wise"', *Feminist Review*, 21: 25–46.

Wright, Elizabeth (ed.) (1992). *Feminism and Psychoanalysis: A Critical Dictionary*. Oxford: Basil Blackwell.

Yeatman, Anna (1984). 'Gender and the Differentiation of Social Life into Public and Domestic Domains', *Social Analysis*, 15: 35–50.

Young, Iris (1990). *Justice and the Politics of Difference*. Princeton: Princeton University Press.

Young, Iris (1994). 'Comments on Selya Benhabib's *Situating the Self*', *New German Critique*, 62: 165–72.

Young, Iris (1997). 'Is Male Gender Identity the Cause of Male Domination?', in D. Tietjens Meyers (ed.), *Feminist Social Thought: A Reader*. London: Routledge.

Žižek, Slavoj (1999). *The Ticklish Subject: The Absent Centre of Political Ontology*. London: Verso.

INDEX

generative paradigm of 4–6,
16–17, 18–19, 20–1,
161–4
symbolic
realm of 29, 35, 43, 132,
138–41, 143–7, 169n,
172n
violence 24, 36–8, 51
Strathern, Marilyn 159
sublimation 138, 147–50
Sztompka, Piotr 160

Thompson, John B. 113
time 4–6, 18–19, 25–6, 27–8,
33–6, 38–40, 45–6, 49,
78–81, 85–9, 110–13,
167n

see also embodiment,
narrative

unconscious 8, 128–9
see also imaginary

VanEvery Jo 94
Violi, Patrizia 82–3

Walby, Sylvia 16, 68, 98, 156
Weir, Allison 100–2
Whitebook, Joel 141–2

Yeatman, Anna 70
Young, Iris 158

Žižek, Slavoj 56, 90, 121, 128